A STORYTELLER IN ZION

A STORYTELLER IN ZION

ESSAYS AND SPEECHES BY

ORSON SCOTT CARD

BOOKCRAFT
SALT LAKE CITY, UTAH

First paperbound printing, 2000.

Visit us at www.deseretbook.com

Library of Congress Catalog Card Number: 93-72419

ISBN 1-57345-808-2

Printed in the United States of America

10 9 8 7 6 5 4 3 2 1 72082-6697

To Scott Kenney
with love, respect, and gratitude

Contents

The Coming of the Nonmembers
1

PART ONE
Some Gospel Views
9

The Book of Mormon—Artifact or Artifice?
13

Sunday Meetings: A Preparation for Work
46

Family Art
49

PART TWO
Moral Storytelling
63

The Problem of Evil in Fiction
69

On Art, Morals, and Morality
99

PART THREE
The Artist in Mormon Society
107

Art as an Act of Charity
111

Sermons in Critical Form
130

Walking the Tightrope
138

Prophets and Assimilationists
149

Science Fiction and the Mormon Religion
156

PART FOUR
Building Zion
163

Consecration: A Law We Can Live With
167

Eugene England and the Lighted Lamp
175

The Hypocrites of Homosexuality
182

Living in Zion
195

Acknowledgments
213

About the Author
216

The Coming of the Nonmembers

Uncle Lamar and Aunt Daverla lived in Orem for seventeen years before they met a nonmember. Their children had never seen a nonmember. Their dog had never pooped on a nonmember's lawn. They were totally unprepared when their next-door neighbors, the Cannons, moved away and a new family moved in.

It started the day the For Sale sign disappeared from the front lawn. Aunt Daverla phoned us and said, "Benulda Miner knows the real estate man's cousin's mother-in-law, and she told us the new family *aren't members.*"

In Utah, you don't ask, "Aren't members of what?" You can be a member of Rotary, Lions, Cub Pack 1134, the Senior Citizens Munch Bunch, and the city council, but if you aren't a Mormon, you aren't a member.

"I wonder if they'll smoke," Aunt Daverla said. My wife, Dandee, said, "If they do, they'll probably go in the bathroom and lock the door," and Aunt Daverla said she was probably right. "But I just don't know. Will it be safe to let the children play with them? What if they have long hair?"

Daverla speculated on drug dealing and orgies in the nonmembers' house for another half hour before we could get off the phone. Then Dandee and I forgot about it, until Thanksgiving brought us down to the big family dinner at Mom's place.

When we got inside the front door, Lamar and Daverla were in the middle of the report on the Nonmember Family, but they were more than willing to start again from the beginning. "We were so pleasantly *surprised,*" Aunt Daverla said, while Uncle Lamar nodded his agreement. "Short hair, no dog, clean children, don't smoke. Everything we could have hoped for. They don't even swear. They could practically be members."

Lamar leaned forward eagerly. "They *hunt,* too," he said, and for about fifteen minutes we heard about the Nonmember Family's twelve-point buck trophy and the three rifles. "They get at least one deer every year," Lamar concluded, beaming with approbation. "They could practically be members."

Which led to the obvious question: "Are you friendshipping them?"

"Friendshipping them!" Daverla exclaimed. "Friendshipping! Why, no sooner did we see that they were all right but what I baked a cake and Lamar went to the garage to gas up the lawnmower. But it was so *disgusting*. Lamar got the mower going and what do you think? Brother Andrews from across the street was already out there, mowing their lawn. And the Nonmember Family lives next door to *us.*"

"And then Daverla goes over there with the cake, and there's the presidency of the Relief Society and the Honeywells from the other side and Sister Johnson from through the block," Lamar said.

Daverla interrupted. "I was so mad I could have spit nails. *Our* next-door neighbor, *our* golden contact, and everybody else wants to muscle in and get all the glory."

It turned out that everybody left a cake, and Lamar mowed the back yard while Brother Andrews mowed the front.

"But it hasn't done any good at all," Daverla concluded, a little miffed.

"Why not? With that kind of fellowship . . ."

"Oh, they're Seventh-day Adventists. We no sooner started talking religion than they whipped out these tracts and started trying to convert *us*. As if we didn't already have the truth. I almost wished I'd kept the cake myself. It was a spice cake with penuche icing, you know."

"I would've liked to have a piece of that cake, all right," said Uncle Lamar. "But, I figure that cake's been chalked up in heaven as good marks for us, even if the Nonmember Family *isn't* interested in the Church."

Then it was time for Thanksgiving dinner, and I've got to admit it, Mom cooks a wonderful turkey, even if her dressing is always wet. Dandee pretended that she could stand candied yams, and then dinner was over and we were getting ready to head back to Salt Lake City when I asked, "What was that Nonmember Family's name, anyway?"

"Oh, Muskoblitz or Moskowitch. Anyway, some Russian name or Polish or Austrian or something. Couldn't pronounce it." And then Uncle Lamar went back to the football game. That was all we heard about the Nonmember Family, but on the way home my wife turned to me and said, "You know something?"

I offered the opinion that I knew several things, and she disagreed.

"No, no honey, I mean you know what I want to do?"

"What?"

"I think it'd be fun to move back to Orem someday."

"Sure," I agreed, "as soon as the kids are old enough to understand."

"But when we go," she insisted, "let's tell everybody we aren't Mormons!"

I kind of liked the idea. After the initial visit, we'd never be bothered by our neighbors again. But then we realized that the first time we went to church the game would be up. Oh well. I guess only nonmembers can get that kind of privacy in Utah.

I wrote this bit of fiction back in 1978, when my wife Kristine and I still lived in Utah. I had completely forgotten I wrote it until an editor from Bookcraft called me up and proposed doing a collection of essays. "I haven't written enough," I said. "Yes you have," he said, and proved it by sending me xeroxes of enough essays to fill a book—along with this story. I removed some of the essays and replaced them with some speeches that he didn't have copies of. The result is the book you have in your hand.

Why should you read it?

I'm not a prophet, and have no special claim to inspired insights. If that's what you want right now, read the scriptures and obey the commandments and pray. This book is no replacement for that.

Nor am I a scholar. I read constantly, I think a lot, but I haven't done any profound original research and I claim no expertise in anything except the one modest skill I use to make a living—that is, I know a bit about how to tell fictional stories. So why don't I just stick to that, let my fiction speak for itself, and not take up space on the shelves of your local Mormon bookstore with a book of essays?

What I know are things that many people know; what I say are things that other people have said. And yet I know from experience that you can hear a thing a hundred times, and not only never understand it, but never even understand that you haven't yet understood it. Then, suddenly, you hear the same thing, but spoken in a different way, or in a different context, or simply by a different person—and lo! The idea that has eluded you for so long suddenly opens up to you, because at last you are ready to receive it, or at last someone has said it in a way that allows you to understand.

So that's what this book is for. There's a chance that when I speak what truth I've learned in my limited experience, there will be readers who have been waiting to hear it in the way I've learned to say it. There will be readers who happen to be open, at this moment, to being touched by the Spirit of understanding.

Of course there will also be others who find no harmony with my way of speaking or thinking, and even some who are offended by my attitudes. They are not wrong; neither am I. We Latter-day Saints are bound together by our commitment to the Church the Lord has established and by our faith that he speaks today through living prophets. Beyond that, there is enormous room for differences among us. Out of charity we do not condemn each other's differences, but rather offer each other the best gifts we have, and receive from all the best gifts they offer. It may be that the gifts I offer are not attractive to you; I am not offended by that. There are many faults in both the gift and the giver, though I can assure you that where I am aware of the fault, I have tried my best to correct it. I will yet learn many things, and the opinions and ideas I have today will certainly be refined and transformed in time, as they have been refined and transformed many times before.

In other words, if you find that I am wrong about something, no one will be surprised, least of all myself. I'm perfectly willing to admit that I don't understand everything, and there are days that I suspect I don't *really* understand anything. I have never yet met anybody who didn't have something to teach me, if I had the wit and meekness to learn.

But I'm pretty sure of one thing: There's bound to be a few things that *you* don't understand, either, and there's a decent chance that I may have learned something that you haven't yet learned. So, likewise, neither of us should be surprised if you do find something of value here, however small. That's what the Church is for, isn't it? So we can pool our scant wisdom and do great works together in the service of the Savior.

There are many senses in which the Church is perfect. One of them is this: The Church perfectly reflects the character of the people who are in it. This has always been true of the Lord's church, and always will be. It happens, though, that the Church is composed of imperfect people, and that means that even an inspired precept can be distorted and misused, and people can be hurt. What do we do about this?

We must do *something*. For we believe that Christ will come again, in the hour when we "look not for him"; it matters a great deal what he finds us doing when he comes. Specifically, I believe he expects us, his church, to have already become a Zion society, a people ready for him to dwell among us. And it is certain that we have not yet achieved that degree of righteousness as a people. Though we have gained ground in some areas, we have lost it in others. Our obedience and love are still imperfect. We have, as a people, fallen into many habits of thought and speech and action that we must overcome before he comes again, so that we will be glad and not ashamed to answer when he asks us what we have been doing with the stewardship he gave us.

We must forgive each other. Sometimes this is hard and takes time, and forgiveness is a skill I haven't perfectly mastered. There are people in the Church who have hurt me that I have not yet forgiven, and there are people I have hurt who have not yet forgiven me. But I think we're all working on it, and becoming better people in the process.

But forgiving each other isn't enough. We also have to teach each other. What good does it do to forgive somebody when you don't also make an effort to help him learn what it was that gave offense? Yes, we treat kindly the young couple whose violation of the commandments has led to a pregnancy out of wedlock. But we also are unflinching in our affirmation of the truth that what they did was wrong in the eyes of God and of the community that they live in. To do any less is to hurt them and every other person in that community who might, from our forgiveness, conclude that no harm was done. We have a sacred responsibility in the Church to point out error even as we love and forgive the individual who erred.

What this comes down to, in practical terms, is that we condemn in general and forgive in particular. (Church courts are another matter, of course—they sometimes have to condemn in particular for the good of the Church as a whole.) I see no inconsistency in my love for good friends who have sinned grievously, in personally holding no ill thoughts toward them because of their struggles with matters of righteousness, while at the same time I condemn the kind of sin that they have committed, warning them and others in general or fictional (and therefore not personal) terms of the harm caused by such violations of good order.

Fiction, in that sense, can be (indeed, always is) merely another kind of pulpit. What the storyteller believes about how the world works, about what is good and important and true and what is evil and distracting and false, will always show up in his stories. And yet stories can be structured in such a way that they entertain even as they teach—the best stories always are, because without that element of entertainment, the audience doesn't stick around long enough to learn. Jesus knew this, and taught in parables. Those of us who have some knack for storytelling are thus following in a worthy tradition when we tell stories that call for correction.

The little story at the head of this essay is slight indeed, and I hope you found at least a little humor in it. Yet the subject matter is serious enough, dealing as it does with the way we too often treat the nonmembers in our midst, befriending them only in order to bring them into our community, and "disappearing" them if they fail to fulfill our hopes. It gives us an appearance of hypocrisy or exploitativeness. I could have written an essay on the subject, but I think that telling that little story makes the point more effectively, if only because many readers who actually act this way are more likely to recognize themselves and realize the need to change when they see it in fiction than when they hear about it in an overt sermon.

That's why my wife and I have started Hatrack River Publications, which is devoted to bringing out Mormon fiction that, while absolutely loyal to the Church and the gospel, nevertheless points out our foibles and weaknesses as a people and points the way toward improvement. Most of the fiction we publish is humorous; most of it is also sometimes painful. And it is a way that people with certain gifts can use those talents for the benefit of the Church.

Unfortunately, I can't rely on the softening effects of fiction in this book. But then, the Savior didn't do *all* his teaching in parables, either. Sometimes you want to speak directly, clearly, passionately. To some of you who are familiar with my fiction, some of these essays may seem a great deal less entertaining—and a great deal more "absolute" than anything in my stories. If you don't enjoy this, I urge you to simply return to my fiction and we can both be content with that. My stories are a far truer indicator of who I am and what I believe. In stories it is ultimately impossible to deceive anyone about either; but in essays and speeches, you will find only what I *believe* that I believe. I hope you will find things of value and truth in this book—but you will not find as much of my true self here as you will in my stories. That is inevitable; it is built into the nature of storytelling as opposed to polemic.

Having warned you so thoroughly, I wonder now if there'll be anyone left to read the rest of this book. I hope there is, and that, armed with grains of salt and much patience, you will go on and give your time and thought to the essays and speeches presented here. Where a speech or essay needs some kind of introduction or commentary, I provide it; otherwise, they stand alone. Of all of them I can say this: I wouldn't have spoken or written about these things if I did not believe in them and care about them and think that an understanding of them could do some good. I hope you find this to be the case for you.

PART ONE

Some Gospel Views

Having told you that I have no special claim to inspiration, why then do I begin by talking about the gospel?

The first item in this section is a commentary on the Book of Mormon, not based upon scholarly research or upon spectacular inspiration, but rather upon my observations after years of study of the Book of Mormon, wrestling with it as the starting point for many works of art. As a science fiction writer I think I have some insights into the nature of the Book of Mormon itself that may be of interest and value; and in fact I made two earlier attempts to deal with this subject, first at a Sunstone symposium near Washington, D.C., many years ago, and more recently in the Greensboro North Carolina Stake, where I was asked to give a series of presentations to members and nonmembers as part of my then calling as a counselor in the stake mission presidency. It is my third attempt, however, given at BYU in 1993, that most fully treats the subject; I have taken the liberty of including or expanding upon ideas that were left out or given short shrift in the single hour I had on that occasion.

The other two items are articles I was assigned to write as part of my work at the *Ensign* magazine when I worked there from May 1976 through the end of December 1977. I would not have presumed to write upon either subject had I not been asked to do so; having been asked, however, I fulfilled the assignment to the best of my ability and offer them again here for whatever value you might find in them.

The Book of Mormon—Artifact or Artifice?

Adapted from a speech given at the BYU Symposium on Life, the Universe, and Everything, February 1993

The Book of Mormon is the most important book in my life. I remember it as one of the earliest things I read, starting with Emma Marr Petersen's children's adaptation. The illustrations in that book still linger in my mind as what black-and-white illustrations should look like. Soon I graduated to the Book of Mormon itself. I've read it many, many times.

It shows up in my style. Anybody who wonders why practically every sentence begins with *and, then, but*—you just have to think of the phrase "And it came to pass," and you will understand where that comes from. You see, if a sentence is important and true, I instinctively feel that it must begin with a conjunction.

But the influence is much deeper than style. It was the Book of Mormon that brought me to BYU as a student. My high school grades were such that I could have taken my pick of schools, but I applied only here, because I intended to become an archaeologist and work on understanding the Book of Mormon. I saw no point in going to any school that did not take the Book of Mormon seriously as an ancient document referring to real-world events.

Later, when I had abandoned the study of archaeology, mostly because I had found out that it was hard work, the Book of Mormon still kept changing my life. I was a theatre student at BYU when I attended a play adaptation of some events in the Book of Mormon. I sat there thinking, "Oh. Oh, she missed the point, she didn't see what's really important in the story." That impelled me to write my own treatment of that same story, which became one of my first produced plays, *The Apostate,* directed by Charles Whitman in the Arena Theatre at BYU. It was that play which launched me on my career as a writer.

For the rest of my time at BYU, half my writing consisted of adapting other Book of Mormon stories into plays. Years after I graduated, I worked on the first six animated adaptations of the Book of Mormon for Living Scriptures. A few years ago, I was called upon by the Brethren to rewrite the Hill Cumorah Pageant. They told me to ignore the existing script, and instead to go back to the Book of Mormon and find a way to shape a clear and coherent story that would present the book's most important themes for an audience of nonmembers. I've been exploring, analyzing, dramatizing this book for a long time.

So, it seemed to me only natural that I should write my *Homecoming* series—*The Memory of Earth, The Call of Earth, The Ships of Earth.* These books are really just another dramatization of the Book of Mormon, only transformed into a science fictional setting, where by fictionalizing it I have the freedom to explore questions of character and society in a way that I couldn't in a more direct adaptation.

Elements of the Book of Mormon have shown up in many of my other works. The massacre at Tippy-Canoe in *Red Prophet,* for instance, clearly is taken from the Book of Mormon. Sometimes my debt to the Book of Mormon is unconscious. Not until Professor Michael Collings pointed it out did I realize that in my first novel, *Hot Sleep,* the naive narrators in the middle of the book were clearly reminiscent of the narrators in the books taken from the small plates of Nephi.

In short, I have explored the Book of Mormon again and again, going back to that deep well to draw water. No matter how much I take from it, the well is still full.

What Is This Book?

The Book of Mormon has its own account of how we got it. Most of us here are familiar with that account. Joseph Smith told us how he got the book. You know the story. An angel appeared in his bedroom three times in one night. Later on, while he was climbing over a fence, it appeared to him again. A most insistent angel!

Following the angel's directions, Joseph Smith went to a nearby hill where he found buried in it an artifact of an ancient civilization—golden plates with words written on them in a language he did not understand.

After four years of annual visits to that hill, Joseph Smith took the golden plates into his possession and proceeded to translate them with divine aid, dictating the words of the book to a scribe. We have witnesses of that process, the testimony of people who participated in the translation. Three witnesses were shown the plates by the angel and testified to the book's divine origin. Another eight witnesses handled the plates and swore that they were physically real.

At the end of the Prophet's translation, he returned the plates to the angel Moroni. Therefore, they are not to be seen among us now.

Either Joseph Smith's account is true, or it isn't. Either the witnesses who said they saw the plates lied, or they didn't.

If the account he gave us is true, then the Book of Mormon must be what it purports to be, which is the record of an ancient people written by an ancient author, and Joseph Smith's role in providing us with the Book of Mormon was solely as translator. Therefore, we should find his influence in the book, or the influence of any other 1820s American, only where we would expect to find a translator's influence: that is, in matters of word choice, consciously or unconsciously linking Book of Mormon events to experiences that he and his American readers could understand, choosing the clearest language he had available to him, fitting ideas he found in the book into existing American concepts as best he could.

Or he did not get the Book of Mormon the way he said, in which case somebody in the 1820s in the United States made it up, and in that case it is fiction, and we should find Joseph Smith's or someone else's influence there *as author.* In that case *all* of the ideas and events in the book should come out of the mind of an 1820s American, and it should reflect faithfully the kind of thing an 1820s American would do in trying to create a record which he was going to pass off as an ancient document.

Scripture . . . Now, if the Book of Mormon is scripture, who wrote it? The first part of it is written by a man named Nephi, probably writing as an older man looking back on his life, explaining to his own people why and how they were chosen by God. It would have been written in the context of many wars against his brothers' people, and therefore would include a great deal of justification of his own people's rightness versus their enemies' wrongness. It would not be an impartial history by any means, or even an impartial autobiography. It's highly selective: It states clearly that it is designed to show how God worked with him and his family. It includes transcriptions of his favorite scriptures and commentary on the ideas that matter most to him. He has a very specific audience with clear recorded purposes in mind.

The next author is Jacob, Nephi's younger brother, who has no memory of Jerusalem and, therefore, less contact with the culture of that city. He's a vigorous disciple of his older brother, he's writing to the people of his own time, and he's also aware of the scriptures' importance to the people of the future.

Then Enos, Jacob's son, gives his personal testimony, but he's not taking that same role as a teacher or leader in his culture. Then we have a group of authors writing with increasing brevity, sometimes as little as a verse: Jarom, Omni, and others following after. They are minor, weak, and dwindling. They amount to virtually nothing, until the last one writes only to justify turning his particular records over to the king, who is the suitable person, in his mind, to receive ancient records.

Which, by the way, is something that would certainly not be a cultural idea available to Joseph Smith. You don't turn ancient records over to kings in the world of the 1820s in

America. Kings would have nothing to do with ancient records. You would turn ancient records over to a *scholar.* We know that that was Joseph Smith's personal attitude, because when he wanted to find support for his translation in order to encourage Martin Harris's continuing support, he sent Harris, *not* to a king or a president or a political leader, but to a scholar.

The next author we meet is Mormon, the dominant author of the text of the Book of Mormon. He's a man who was a general since his youth, a leader of armies, a man of war, and a man of God. We should expect to see reflections of that in the text. He is watching his people collapse and decay, and no doubt wondering about the mechanisms that cause nations to collapse and decay. For much of his life he is forbidden to preach to his own people, though he longs to do so. Instead he devotes his time to collecting and abridging ancient writings, but the resulting writings will probably reflect his desire to preach.

From the Words of Mormon through to Mormon's own book, he abridged old historical records, prophecies, biographies, speeches written by other people. You will find in his text both abridgments and summaries of other people's writings, and therefore we should find traces of *their* attitudes and feelings in the book. In addition, we will find the voices of those whose works he includes whole, or at least the voices of those who purport to have written down what they said. We'll find his priorities and interests reflected in his selection of things to include.

Then we meet Mormon's son Moroni as an author. He writes relatively little, but he is a prophet and military leader in his own right. He had helped in his father's work and in fact completed Mormon's eponymous book. We may also have encountered his voice here and there earlier in the text without knowing it. He continued writing in solitude after his father's death. The book ends with his testimony, which looks almost entirely to our time, and he is the one who, resurrected, returned to lead Joseph Smith to the plates.

We also have another important author, Ether, but we only have his writings as abridged by Moroni, and Ether's writings are themselves an abridgment and a summary of earlier records from a culture completely unrelated to the cultural traditions from which the rest of the Book of Mormon arose. We should find traces of that earlier culture, though it should be triple-filtered through the perceptions and concerns of the abridgers, Ether and Moroni, and the translator, Joseph Smith.

We're talking about a seriously complex artifact here.

If the Book of Mormon is scripture, then these are the authors of the book.

. . . Or Hoax. *If* the Book of Mormon is literature, then some American in the 1820s, most probably Joseph Smith, actually set out to fake a document that would fool us into thinking that all these other guys wrote it, reflecting the concerns of at least three different cultures, none of them particularly similar to the culture of frontier America in its fifth decade.

The project of faking up the Book of Mormon is what I'm going to talk about here, because it's very much like what we science fiction writers do. Most of the time, though, we don't pretend to be creating a document from another culture. Instead, American science fiction writers make it very plain that we are 20th-century Americans writing to 20th-century Americans. Nevertheless, occasionally a science fiction writer or a fantasy writer *does* write a document that in itself purports to be from another culture. And whether the text pretends to have been written from within another culture or not, most science fiction presents cultures that no one has ever seen, histories that no one else can verify. We write about made-up lands and made-up cultures. If the Book of Mormon were fiction, Joseph Smith or someone else must have done the same—made up a culture that no one else has ever seen.

Writing something that purports to be an artifact of another culture is the most complicated, difficult kind of science fiction, because not only is it *about* strange things, it must also in itself *be* a strange thing. And when you have not one but several different narrators with different rhetorical stances, it becomes even more difficult. There are different perspectives, different personalities, and the culture must change across time, so that writers from the culture early on must somehow have differences from writers in that culture later on.

So we're talking about a very tough project, one which is rarely attempted and which is almost *never* attempted under circumstances where the author actually tries to pass it off as a genuine document. Even those of us who write science fiction publish it with the word *fiction* somewhere on the cover. Our name is on it as author, and we expect to get credit for our inventiveness. We don't try to say we *found* it.

There is a historical precedent, however. In the 1760s an ancient Scottish poet named Ossian was "discovered" by a man named James Macpherson, who supposedly translated this work of ancient Celtic poetry which he found. In his own time, his work was taken very seriously as an ancient text. It was an era when people loved the idea of finding ancient manuscripts, especially manuscripts native to the British Isles. When they praised the poems, they praised Ossian, not Macpherson. It was in an era when new work was not respected as much as old work, so if you could find a way to put out new work as old work, you'd get much more favorable attention for it. Macpherson was not a particularly good poet—but Ossian supposedly came from a more primitive time, and therefore *his* poetry was remarkably sophisticated for the time it was supposedly written.

Macpherson produced exactly what people of his time expected or desired ancient Celtic poetry to be. But it also happened to be deeply, hopelessly wrong. It took only a little while before the fraud was exposed. Though most critics accepted Ossian, Samuel Johnson accused Macpherson of forgery during his lifetime; Macpherson never did refute that charge or provide the originals. Yet he remained a Member of Parliament until his death in 1796. Today, of course, the press would have seized upon Johnson's charges and hounded Macpherson to an early grave. It was a more courteous age.

Today, though, when you look at the works of Ossian you can clearly see that this is the work of an 18th-century British writer. It has nothing to do with what you'd expect to find from an ancient Scottish writer. It's an obvious hoax, good enough only to fool people in a fundamentally ignorant time.

Cultural Confession

Joseph Smith's project, if it was a fraud, was far more ambitious than Macpherson's; a much longer, more extensive work, with multiple authors. We're talking about somebody jumping off a cliff here, folks. His work should proclaim itself to be a phony on every page today. This is because every storyteller, no matter how careful he is, will inadvertently confess his own character and the society he lives in. He can make every conscious effort, he can be the best-educated scholar you could possibly find, but if he tries to write something that is not of his own culture he will give himself away with every unconscious choice he makes. Yet he'll never know he's doing it because it won't occur to him that it could be any other way.

Even the best science fiction writers make this mistake all the time, but we forgive it because we don't expect any better. They're not really pretending to be translating a genuine document of another culture. They're looking for readers, not believers.

You can spot, immediately, the decade in which almost any science fiction story was written. Any one of you here could do it. The conventions of language alone will give it away. The style of writing that was prevalent in the 1950s is completely different from what you expect in the post-1960s world of science fiction. Anybody who is writing after William Gibson will have been bent by *Neuromancer.* We'll see the influences of each era, because the accepted mode of storytelling has changed.

Furthermore, we find preoccupations with contemporary issues. Science fiction of the 1950s invariably has some element that refers to the fear of Communism or Nazism. In the 1960s and 1970s we find lots of references to rebellious counter-culture groups, libertarianism starts popping up seriously, and we find a lot of drug-culture stories, reflecting concerns and values that were virtually unknown earlier.

The level of knowledge of science will also change across time in science fiction. Nobody's writing stories about breathing the atmosphere of Venus anymore.

Most important are the cultural assumptions. Let's step outside science fiction for a moment. How many of you have seen old episodes of "I Love Lucy"? The relationship between a husband and wife in that show, between males and females in general, is deeply offensive, to me at least. Actually, it was deeply offensive to me even in the fifties. As a child I never liked Lucy because I thought she was an idiot, and I really never liked her husband because I thought he treated her like a jerk—but I had a different standard of what a husband and wife should be than the rest of American culture, apparently, because I *never* saw the series criticized on those grounds at the time.

Nevertheless, even as recently as "Bewitched" we find ludicrous remnants of a pre-feminist culture; and yet the writers writing in that time had no concept that they were giving away the fact that they were writing in the fifties or sixties. They would never have dreamed that they had better change the way they treat women in their fiction in order to make sure that people from the seventies still could understand their work and its context. It didn't cross their minds because it didn't occur to them that the relationship between men and women could possibly be any other way.

The same thing is clear in fiction from the 1930s and 1940s, wherever the writers depict the relationship between blacks and whites in America. Even people who would have thought themselves very liberal, open-minded, tolerant, non-racist people nevertheless put blacks in a social role with attitudes that would be unthinkable in fiction today. You know when you're reading something from the thirties and forties because of the perfectly blithe and innocent way in which these writers keep blacks "in their place." At the time, it didn't cross their minds that there could ever be a time when white people would seriously think of black people being their intellectual and social equals. And as for blacks and whites marrying each other and remaining acceptable to other people—that was unthinkable, even among the most liberal.

Even now, today, we have assumptions that we do not *think* to question. Assumptions about property ownership, for example, which are really not that widespread through time—but our fiction invariably assumes that people own the things they own and will continue to own them for quite some time. We even have the ludicrous assumption that after we're dead we still have the right to control the disposition of our property and pass it along to our heirs. What a silly notion, really—but it's not questioned in our fiction. (Of course, now that I've questioned it, you'll be aware of it—but even at this moment some of you are incapable of understanding how property could be handled any other way; you are so deeply involved in American culture of the 1990s you can't even comprehend the Doctrine and Covenants.)

We make other assumptions. For instance, we assume that someone's job is somehow tied to his identity. Who are you? I'm an engineer. What is he? He's a doctor. In many other cultures it would be unthinkable to answer these questions in terms of career. The answers would refer to family, tribe, city, or caste. What would your *occupation* have to do with anything? But stories produced by contemporary Americans don't question the assumption that career is the most important distinguishing feature of character.

We make assumptions about education, about what formal education means, about how necessary it is, about what it's for, about who should get it. We make assumptions about family relationships and how important a particular family relationship will be in our lives. In America today, very little fiction actually includes family members outside the immediate family in any kind of important role. A cousin? Why in the world would cousins come up in the story? And if a grandparent is living in the same house with the main character, it is regarded as unusual; it is commented upon.

Most contemporary fiction writers don't even have questions about the fundamental morality of our culture, even though it has changed drastically in many ways over the past thirty years. We take a lot of things for granted that are not necessarily taken for granted in other cultures. How much fiction have you read lately in which the author does *not* assume that two people who are mutually attracted will sleep together at the earliest opportunity? And if they *don't* sleep together, it is only because of loyalty to an existing relationship, never because of any moral barrier to unmarried sexual congress.

The Book of Mormon, *if* it is a science fiction work, *if* it is an artifact of the 1820s, should be thick with similar cultural clues; 1820s America should leap out of every page, exactly the way 1950s America leaps out of every minute of every episode of "I Love Lucy."

Language

At the language and word-choice level, of course, the Book of Mormon, as a translated document, should be pure Joseph

Smith. It should reflect what a man of his level of education in 1820s America thinks scripture should sound like. And of course we have exactly the ersatz King James Version voice that the Prophet knew the translation would have to have if it were to be taken as scripture by the people he was going to offer it to. Fake or genuine, the Book of Mormon would need *that.* And, fake or genuine, the Prophet's attempt at old-fashioned formal English should reveal his lack of education—which it does, with numerous grammatical errors and misuses of archaic forms, many of which survive even in current editions of the Book of Mormon.

But it's no surprise that the translator repeatedly errs, because this is not his natural speaking voice. No one speaks this kind of language around him. He doesn't understand the grammar, and so grammatical errors are thick on the ground. Those who believe, like David Whitmer, that the translation appeared word for word on the Urim and Thummim are ripe for disillusionment—or else they are accusing God of some really embarrassing grammatical errors. This is ultimately why David Whitmer ended up outside the Church—he refused to accept the idea that Joseph Smith could edit revelations previously given, precisely because Whitmer believed God gave them to him word for word. But Whitmer's view of translation was wrong. However the process of inspiration worked, it could only produce language that already existed in Joseph Smith's mind. Whether the Book of Mormon is a fraud or a genuine translated book, it will reflect Joseph Smith's language.

So the words are definitely used as 1820s Americans would understand them, or misunderstand them, especially an 1820s American of Joseph Smith's educational level. To a degree they even reflect some of his personal style—but not entirely. As with any translation, there should be word patterns, word orders, idiomatic expressions in the original language that survive translation, that bend the translator's language into new forms and directions. So in the Book of Mormon we should expect to find foreign and alien word patterns along with Joseph Smith's effort to sound scriptural. Much better scholars than I have already explored exactly these elements in Joseph Smith's translation, and I have no intention of trying to move into an area so far from my own expertise. (As a science fiction writer, when I do this sort of thing I fake it mercilessly. I make no effort beyond the most cursory to try to make my narrators speak differently from myself.)

There are many areas apart from language, however, where *only* a science fiction writer or a very perceptive science fiction reader is likely to know how very difficult it is—impossible, really—to tell a story without confessing the author's own culture.

American Culture and the Book of Mormon

If the Book of Mormon is a fake, what should we expect an 1820s American to put into this book?

Lost Tribes. One thing we should definitely expect is exactly what most people who haven't read it assume the Book of Mormon *is.* They assume that it's a book about the ten lost tribes, because that's what Joseph Smith's culture would definitely have produced. It was in the air. Speculation about the Indians being descended from the lost tribes of Israel was common. Why wouldn't Joseph Smith have followed that line of speculation? It's hard to imagine why an 1820s American would come up with some ludicrous story about someone escaping from Judah in 600 B.C. It has nothing to do with anything that matters in American religious culture of the time, while the ten lost tribes were an obsessive topic at the time. Yet it isn't a book about the ten lost tribes. And here's the kicker. If Joseph Smith had been deliberately flouting expectations, he would have made a point within the text about how this is *not* a story of the lost tribes. Yet, contrary to all expectations, the lost tribes are barely hinted at; they have almost nothing to do with the story, negatively or positively.

Women. Another thing we should definitely expect in an 1820s book is a love interest. This is no joke. Biography and history always focused on love interests in that era. Even the Bible has plenty of love-interest stories—Ruth and Boaz, Joseph and Mary, Moses and Zipporah, Abram and Sarai, Isaac and Rebekah, Jacob and Rachel, David and Bathsheba, Solomon and the queen of Sheba—and in Joseph Smith's era, all these stories were interpreted with powerful emphasis on romantic love. Women occupied a very important role in the stories being told in America in the 1820s. No contemporary feminist would approve of the role women played—but they were there, and they mattered. All heroic deeds were done *for* women, to obtain the love of a good woman. We have the troubadours to thank for that. The romantic tradition was very much alive in Joseph Smith's time.

Unfortunately women are virtually absent from the Book of Mormon. When they do manage to show up, they are rarely named. There are only three women who are actually of the culture of the Book of Mormon who are given names. One is Sariah, the mother of Nephi. Another is a harlot named Isabel, and the third is a servant woman named Abish.

None of the queens who show up in the story are mentioned by name. Only one of these writers ever mentions his own wife, and when women do show up in a specific role they're still almost never named. Nephi did not even bother to mention the name of the woman who saved his life by pleading for him in the desert. (A lot of people leap to the conclusion that this must have been the woman who ended up marrying Nephi. My own feeling is that Laman would hardly have listened to the pleading of *Nephi's* wife-to-be. It seems far more likely to me that the woman who pleaded for him was *Laman's* intended. The very fact that Nephi didn't name her supports this, I think, because, while he had to include this woman in his story, he couldn't very well point out that it was the woman who ended up marrying Laman. Laman is the king of the bad guys when Nephi is writing his account, and Laman's wife is presumably queen. Nephi didn't spend much time in his account giving credit to his enemies for their virtuous actions. Of course, none of this is proof—but it's at least an intriguing possibility.)

The way women are treated in the Book of Mormon is not even remotely the way women were regarded and treated in the 1820s in the United States. If you doubt that, you have only to look at the way that Mormon women were treated in the history written by B. H. Roberts, or in the Documentary History of the Church, which is more a product of that time.

It is telling, perhaps, that the only Book of Mormon culture in which mothers play an important role is not the culture of the writers of the book—not Nephite culture. Rather when two thousand young soldiers give credit to their mothers for having taught them courage and righteousness, they are products of *Lamanite* culture. And, again, it is within *Lamanite* culture where the queen of the Lamanites plays an important role in the conversion of her people, and where a servant named Abish, hoping to motivate her fellow Lamanites to believe in God's power, calls the people together to see the Lamanite king and queen who lie in a trance, overwhelmed by the Spirit. Remove these Lamanite cultural expressions from the story, and you find the Book of Mormon quite startling in its omission of women from the events of Nephite history. This is quite foreign to attitudes in Joseph Smith's culture. And while the Book of Mormon attitude toward women *is* perfectly acceptable in many other cultures in world history, they are not cultures the Prophet would have known of.

Awareness of the Audience. But the most telling confessions are little, tiny, unnoticeable choices, because that's where even the most brilliant faker will give himself away. He will make his invented culture different from the culture he lives in—but it will only be different *where he has thought of it.* The Book of Mormon should be an American story except where the author of the hoax thought of making the culture different. Every element of More's *Utopia* and Swift's *Gulliver's Travels* and Defoe's *Robinson Crusoe* is presented in light of English culture of the author's time. Wherever the foreign land has not been made deliberately different from England, it is the same; and where it *is* different, the difference is clearly pointed out and commented upon. Of course, since these works are written from the point of view of a character in the story who is a contemporary Englishman, the narrative *should* point up the differences. But there should be far more differences in the first place; it is absurd how English these foreign lands turn out to be.

The author of an invented culture is going to be proud of his creation. It is almost impossible not to flaunt one's most fascinating ideas, to make them important plot points so that the audience can't possibly miss them. Unfortunately, if the Book of Mormon is a hoax, the author is astonishingly humble. The very cleverest cultural differences are not pointed up; on the contrary, they are often concealed so that most readers are completely unaware of them, and even cite them as examples of *similarities* to 1820s American culture.

Even the humblest and most self-effacing of authors, however, are incapable of completely forgetting the contemporary audience. Even when the narrator is supposedly a member of the strange culture, the author will still throw in those little explanations that will be necessary for a contemporary audience to understand the culture which he's presenting. Since the author has invented the strange culture, he is keenly aware of all of the differences, all the things that will be hard for his readers to understand. He will make sure that the cultural context is explained. He may be very clever about it, but the explanation will be there.

But if it's a genuine document, those differences will be almost invisible, because the writer won't think that it could possibly be any other way and, therefore, it won't occur to him that it needs any explanation. "I Love Lucy" episodes never stopped to explain, "By the way, the husband is the head of the home and has the authority to tell his wife what to do, just as if she were a child." They assume that the audience will know that. They assume that the audience doesn't need a defense of Ricky's spanking Lucy. "By the way, this isn't wife abuse." The need for such an explanation doesn't occur to them.

However, the Book of Mormon is a complicated document. Mormon is abridging documents that come from many generations before him. Just as there are cultural differences between 1950 and 1990, there will be times when Mormon, writing in the later fourth century, is aware of cultural changes since the time of Alma, for instance, four centuries before. So there *will* be times when he explains culture. However, by and large he will explain those cultural differences, not to *us*, but rather in terms that would clarify them to people of his *own* time. And while Mormon will probably explain things that seem strange to *him* from the earlier documents that he's abridging, it won't occur to him to explain things that still seem perfectly normal to him.

Judges. So—does the author of the Book of Mormon explain things that an American audience of the 1820s would need to have explained, and in terms they would understand? Hardly. Let's look at just some of the most obvious things, some of the places where people *think* Joseph Smith blew it. For example, when Mosiah gives up his throne, the reign of the judges begins, and the judges are chosen "by the voice of the people." This is automatically taken by the critics of the Book of Mormon as proof that Joseph Smith, living in a democracy, had to show American democracy as the ideal government.

Think again. The resemblances between the reign of the judges and American democracy are superficial at best. Mormon, living in a time when judges apparently do *not* rule, explains what *his* culture would need to have explained—but does not comment at all upon the very significant ways that the judges differ from American democracy. The judges may be in some sense chosen by the will of the people, but look at how it actually works. In Joseph Smith's time there was much talk about the Constitutional division of the executive, legislative, and judicial powers. But in the Book of Mormon, the judge not only judges people but also enforces the law and directs the gathering of taxes and supplies and sends them in support of the armies. He enforces traditional law, but when new laws are needed, the judge makes them! Where in American life of his time would Joseph Smith have seen this?

How are these judges selected? We hear of almost no contested elections. On the contrary, judges seem to nominate their successors. With few exceptions, the judge serves until death, and is usually succeeded by a son or brother, or by a member of a family that has previously held the judgeship. Except for the Adamses, there were no dynasties in Joseph Smith's America.

The judges actually function as elected kings. The old pattern of government still endured; they just had a different method of choosing the guy in charge. Mormon pointed out the *difference,* which meant he stressed the election of the judges by the voice of the people, never questioning that authority should stay in only a few aristocratic families and that judges should have monarchical powers. Far from being a mistake in the Book of Mormon, this is one of the places where the Book of Mormon makes it clear that it does *not* come from 1820s American culture. Even the best of hoaxers would have made the judges far more American—or would have avoided hinting at democracy at all.

Lineage. When we do find social classes and political divisions in the Book of Mormon, they seem to reflect patterns that would be alien to anything Joseph Smith was familiar with. To Joseph Smith, social classes were based entirely on money, which was displayed in the form of property. Where money is the basis of social distinction in the Book of Mormon, it is never associated with land, but rather with fine clothing. This is entirely consistent with Mesoamerica, but hardly a pattern Joseph Smith would have known.

When social conflict comes in the Book of Mormon, it seems to follow lineage rather than economic distinctions. A common pattern in the Caribbean basin was for an invading tribe to establish themselves as a permanent ruling class over the indigenous tribe, as the Taino of Haiti did. This seems to be the hidden pattern within the Book of Mormon culture. The Nephites seem to have been a ruling class superimposed on the underlying Mulekite population of Zarahemla, and as their influence spread, they continued this pattern of bringing indigenous people under the rule of a Nephite aristocracy. The Zoramites seem to have done the same, so that the division between the Zoramites and the poor is very clearly drawn. The poor are ruled by the Zoramites, but they are not Zoramites themselves.

In Ammonihah, Amulek asserts that he is a descendant of Nephi. This seems to be important, though it would hardly be so if *everyone* was descended from Nephi. But perhaps the distinction is clearest in the struggle between "king-men" and "freemen." This is thought by many of Joseph Smith's critics to be based on the American Revolution, but if anything it is the opposite—an effort on the part of an old aristocracy to reassert its primacy over the new judges. The America that Joseph Smith knew had no hereditary class that large numbers of people thought had the right to rule. Even in England, a culture the Prophet was probably marginally familiar with, no group of nobles could possibly have assembled a popular army that would seek to bring back kingly rather than parliamentary rule. But Zarahemla had a clan, a lineage, that could command enormous popular support—the old ruling family of the Mulekites. The Nephite kings had abandoned their right to rule and had turned over the government to elected judges. But the indigenous people of Zarahemla would remember that they had once had kings of their own, before these strangers came from the land of Nephi. And they knew who the king should be. So even though the Book of Mormon calls it a war between king-men and freemen—which is how it would certainly appear to those on the side of the freemen, as the writers of the Book of Mormon accounts certainly were—it might have seemed to the king-men themselves to be a struggle between the ancient native tradition and the ruling class, which had surrendered its legitimacy by giving up the throne. After all, the Nephite kings had only ruled for three generations in Zarahemla.

This view makes the Book of Mormon story much clearer and seems to fit the cultural patterns in the book. On the other hand, the American Revolution provides no useful analogy and doesn't fit the facts in the book. Yet if the Book of Mormon were a hoax, this alien social pattern would surely have been pointed out and clarified so that the 1820s American reader couldn't possibly miss it. Instead, it is simply taken for granted by the author, so that it can easily be overlooked by the reader who isn't looking for alien social patterns. Neither Mormon nor the writers whose works he abridged would even think to explain the relationships among tribes and lineages, because to them those things were obvious. For an analogy, you might look at the mysteries of Tony Hillerman. His stories are set on the Navaho reservation of Arizona and New Mexico, yet he feels no need to stop and explain to the American reader that the Navahos were once an independent nation, which was confined to a reservation by the U.S. government. He certainly does not go through the whole history of the relationship between Native Americans and the European invaders. Likewise, how many essays and articles are written about poverty among blacks in American cities today without bothering to go through the whole history of slavery, emancipation, segregation, the African-American migration to the cities of the North, and the struggle for civil rights?

In a longer history of America, of course, these themes would be dealt with, precisely because they have changed over time. In fact, because of the rapidity of change in our culture, we have a tendency to explain a lot more than historians from earlier eras. Even so, how many histories of important events in

American history do you think could be written without a single mention of drive-in movies, microwave ovens, and hand-held calculators? We ignore what we take for granted, just as the writers of the Book of Mormon did. When, after the birth of Christ, the Nephite society broke down completely, people immediately lapsed into tribal organizations—Nephites, Jacobites, Josephites, and so on. But in all the years since the Nephites first organized themselves as a nation, we have had not a single mention of those tribes other than the ruling Nephites themselves. We might have thought that *all* the people were Nephites. And yet those tribal organizations persisted throughout the entire six hundred years of Nephite society and were available to provide a skeletal social organization when the rule of law broke down. So the hoaxer who was writing the Book of Mormon was so brilliant that he not only maintained this shadow organization of society until it was needed in the plot just before King Jacob, but also deliberately did not mention it, in keeping with the way history would be written by someone within that culture.

Speculation on Zarahemla. Let me offer an aside on the matter of Zarahemla and the Mulekites. Much has been made of the statement by King Zarahemla that his people were descended from the youngest son of King Zedekiah. Extraordinary and completely unconvincing efforts have been made to find such a son, overlooked by the Babylonian captors of Jerusalem; just as much effort has been devoted to explaining how a good Jaredite name like Mulek could show up in the family of an Israelite king. But is this really necessary?

In Mesoamerican culture, every ruling class had to assert an ancient ancestor who was a god or, at the very least, a king in an admired culture. Whoever ruled in the Valley of Mexico always had to claim to be descended from or heir of the Toltecs. Rival Mayan cities would play at ancestral one-upmanship. Imagine, now, the vigorous and dangerous Nephites, coming down the valley of the Sidon River from the highlands of Guatemala. King Zarahemla is negotiating with King Mosiah. Mosiah tells him of his ancestry, of course, and the story of how God led Lehi and Nephi out of Jerusalem at the time when Zedekiah was king of Israel.

To Mosiah, what he is doing is bearing his testimony and

asserting the divine guidance that he receives as the legitimate king of a chosen people. To Zarahemla, what he is doing is claiming that his descent from a prophet gives him the right to rule over the people of Zarahemla and displace him from the kingship. So what does Zarahemla do? Well, Mosiah admits that his ancestors were *not* kings in Israel. So Zarahemla picks his most noble ancestor, Mulek, and then declares him to be the son of that last king of Israel. Thus if anybody has the right to rule over anybody, it's Zarahemla who has the right to rule over Mosiah and his people. But Mosiah kindly points out that if Zarahemla and his people are descended from Israelites, they certainly seem to have forgotten the language and writing, and therefore have obviously degenerated from the high culture of Israel. The Nephites, on the other hand, have preserved a writing system that no one else uses, and which Zarahemla can't read. They have a history accounting for every year since they arrived in America, which Zarahemla of course cannot produce.

In the end, whatever negotiation there was ended up with Zarahemla bowing out of the kingship and his people becoming subject to rule by the Nephites. But the story of Mulek served a very useful purpose even so—it allowed the people to merge, not with the hostility of conquerors over the conquered, though in fact that is what the relationship fundamentally was, but rather with the idea of brotherhood. They were *all* Israelites. Thus no one had any reason to question the Mulek story, because while it failed in its original purpose, to allow Zarahemla to prevail over Mosiah, it still served the valuable function of uniting the newly combined nations as a single tribe. It wasn't completely successful, of course, or there wouldn't have been a later revolt of king-men against Nephite freemen, but considering that the people of Zarahemla outnumbered the people of Mosiah by quite a bit, the Mulek story may well have contributed to the ultimate victory of the judges in that struggle.

If this speculation is true, it does not imply that the Book of Mormon is somehow false. No one in the Book of Mormon ever claims that the story of Mulek came to anybody by inspiration. The source is never more than Zarahemla's assertion during his negotiations with Mosiah. That Mormon and other writers *believed* the story does not prove it true or false; it simply proves that it was part of the Nephite culture. And if my speculation is right, and Mulek was no more a son of Zedekiah than I am, we are spared the confusion of trying to reconcile this account with the utter lack of convincing evidence that Zedekiah had a boy named Mulek who escaped the Babylonians without generating a vast amount of Jewish tradition looking for the return of the lost son of the last king of Judah. We don't have to account for a migration to America led by the Lord but without the same kind of preparation and commandments given to Lehi and Nephi. We don't have to account for the fact that we think of America as being the inheritance of Manasseh and Ephraim, while in fact two-thirds of the Nephites would have been descended from Judah—which to my mind, at least, would make hash of the literality of the application of the parable of the stick of Joseph and the stick of Judah to the Book of Mormon and the Bible.

But this is only speculation, and if I'm wrong, and there really was a Mulek led to America by the Lord, I'm not going to lose my testimony over it! I just think it's something to think about, a possibility to consider.

Instant Cities. Joseph Smith lived in a place where new settlements had sprung up in the wilderness, and he was quite familiar with what it took. Americans of his time and place knew perfectly well the difference between a settlement, a village, a town, and a city. They knew from hard experience exactly what it took to get from wilderness to city—how many years, how many settlers.

So why is it that when Captain Moroni is trying to secure the Nephite borders, he founds *cities* left and right? Cities that are instantly fortified and populated, seemingly without any kind of migration of settlers from the heartland of the Nephites? Joseph Smith knew the word *fort,* and knew perfectly well that a military commander trying to secure hostile country would not found cities—he would build forts and leave garrisons in them.

But in Mesoamerican culture, particularly in the jungles where the Mayans built their cities, there were always small villages and settlements in the wilderness, families on their own; and an ambitious king looking to expand could very easily move into a new territory, gather together a lot of isolated and vulnerable settlers, and unite them into a city. No settlers were needed from outside. The people were already there. They simply gathered together to create public works—temples, in Mayan times; but in Moroni's case, fortifications for defense. The cities didn't require large garrisons, since the newly gathered people became citizen soldiers. And many people would gladly accept the overlordship of the nation that gathered them and made a city out of them. It gave them greater safety, a sense of identity, and bonds with a great nation and desirable culture, not to mention a powerful religion.

Nobody in 1820s America knew anything about this. Yet Captain Moroni goes through the wilderness building cities exactly as Mayans could and did. And the author of the Book of Mormon didn't even make a big deal about it—just took it for granted as being the way the world worked. Of course you can build instant cities in the wilderness without bringing in outside settlers. So it seemed to Mormon. But could it possibly have seemed that way to Joseph Smith?

Lawyers. The appearance of lawyers in the Book of Mormon is assumed by many to be proof that this is an American artifact. After all, Joseph Smith and his family had plenty of reason to have a low opinion of lawyers, and the references to lawyers in the Book of Mormon are hardly flattering.

But there is nothing uniquely American about lawyers. The Romans had lawyers, too, and Roman lawyers were a lot more like what the Book of Mormon showed than any American lawyers that Joseph Smith was acquainted with. That is, a lawyer like Zeezrom seemed to be effective, not because of more skillful manipulation of law, but because of his persuasiveness and personal influence. He would take someone under his protection and speak as personal advocate. With Zeezrom on your side, you would win, not because he understood the law, but because of his rhetoric and his reputation for power. Furthermore, the prosecution of Alma and Amulek seemed to originate with the lawyers themselves as the complainants, while Alma and Amulek had no defense attorney, but rather spoke for themselves. It doesn't follow the American pattern.

Naming. In fact, the only thing that makes Zeezrom and his ilk seem American is the fact that Joseph Smith translated the Nephite word for the role they played in Nephite society as the English word *lawyer*. And this is exactly right. If Joseph Smith was receiving the pure knowledge of what the Book of Mormon authors meant as they wrote, he would still have to put it down in English. In a few rare cases, the idea he was trying to translate had no English equivalent, and so we find cureloms and cumoms. But most of the time there was some English word that came to Joseph Smith, a word that was close enough to convey the idea. As with all translation, though, the words are *never* exact and never can be. It is the most correct translation possible, but a perfect translation is not possible. So for Joseph Smith to apply the word *lawyer* to an advocate in a legal system that was not very close to the American legal system can be misleading, but it is still the most correct possible translation, given the language that the Prophet had available to him at the time.

In fact, the very lack of exotic names supports the genuineness of Joseph Smith's translation. Science fiction writers and critics are quite aware of a long tradition of what James Blish called "shmeerps." Blish pointed out how silly it was that most science fiction writers, when trying to show an alien fauna, would produce a creature that looked like a rabbit and acted like a rabbit and was treated like a rabbit, and yet was called a "shmeerp." This is ludicrous, of course. People migrating to a new land with strange plants and animals will use familiar names for the new creatures. Thus the English immigrants to America called the bison "buffaloes" and referred to maize as "Indian corn" and finally just "corn," even though in England that word had been a generic term for grain. The English felt no need to come up with new names for items that were "close enough."

Surely the Nephites followed the same pattern, using old words for new objects. Thus, if in fact there were no horses in America at the time of the Book of Mormon, the Hebrew word for *horse* could still quite readily be applied to some other animal that functioned like a horse. Furthermore, the language Mormon wrote in may well have been an ideographic language, in which case it would hardly matter what the *spoken* word for a particular animal was, as long as Nephite writers had agreed to use the old "horse" ideograph to refer to that animal. Thus it is no more surprising that the word *horse* appears in the Book of Mormon than that the word *buffalo* was used in a nation where there were no buffaloes but only bison.

The funny thing, though, is that most science fiction writers *still* get it wrong, *still* come up with dozens of needless and often unpronounceable alien or "modern-sounding" names for commonplace objects. We've had computers for two generations now, and no one has yet felt a need to call them "puters," for instance—and yet I still find brand-new science fiction novels that come up with a stupid futuristic name for computers. When a science fiction writer wants to show a futuristic book, which is read digitally, he'll often come up with some fancy new name for it. It doesn't seem to occur to him that futuristic books will be called—get this—"books." After all, when we wanted a name for the thing we drive around in, we called it a "car," even though automobiles were quite different from railroad cars. The word *automobile* also survived, of course, because English is a language that loves redundancy. But think of how often you talk about getting the kids into the auto. The common word is the word that already existed and which was simply applied to the new thing. And we Americans are a people accustomed to new word coinages and technical innovations that demand new language. Most cultures are not so open to new language, and most languages are not so open to borrowing and coinages. They tend to apply old language to new situations.

We science fiction writers have generations of experience to guide us, and we still can't get it right. The author of the Book of Mormon, if it's a hoax, managed to get it right—even in cases where getting it right looks *wrong* to most people, who haven't thought it through. This is an important point. The natural tendency with storytellers who are trying to create an alien culture is to come up with all kinds of new words to show how strange this culture really is—but the author of the Book of Mormon didn't follow this almost universal pattern. Instead, he did something so sophisticated that even those who do this sort of thing for a living still don't usually get it right.

Of course, it can be argued that the hoaxer who was making up the Book of Mormon was so naive that it didn't occur to him that he was creating an alien society and so he didn't bother with new names. But this is obviously not the case—if he was that naive, he wouldn't have come up with an alien culture in the first place. His Nephites and Lamanites would have been culturally white Americans and North American Indians, which they definitely are not.

Great Spirit. Speaking of cowboys and Indians, why don't we see much more of the 1820s view of American Indians? Where is the Happy Hunting Ground? Where is the teepee or wigwam? Where are the moccasins and deerskins, the canoes, the peace pipes? What are we doing with cities instead of villages? Why don't we have any explanation of the great Indian mounds? In short, where is James Fenimore Cooper?

The only time we get anything that sounds like the 1820s white-man view of North American Indians is when Lamoni and Ammon speak of a Great Spirit. This may simply be the way Joseph Smith translated Lamoni's word for *God,* thinking, of course, as he did, of North American Indian beliefs. Thus it could be a matter of word choice. But I'm inclined to believe that it is a fair translation of the concept of God that Lamoni believed in; certainly it is not inconsistent with Mesoamerican beliefs, where a Great Spirit that was the God above all gods seems to have been an available belief.

Transportation. In the Book of Mormon nobody rides anywhere. Think about it. I don't have to explain to you about airplanes when I say I flew here, but I would certainly say that I flew here. People in Joseph Smith's day rode everywhere they could—on either a horse or a wagon. When they took a long journey on foot, they said so, because it was remarkable. But no one in the Book of Mormon rides anywhere. How did Joseph Smith know to keep his made-up Nephites and Lamanites on foot—and how did he keep himself from ever pointing out the fact?

Networks and Relationships. Today we use jobs and school for our networks of relationship. In ancient Rome, it was patrons and clients. In the Book of Mormon it was extended kinship groups. We see clear traces of that in Amulek and in the way that the families of the prophets are treated over the years. Lineage is the first relationship you assert. Family is the first guide to a man's worthiness to rule. Again, this doesn't match anything that Joseph Smith would be familiar with. Family was important in 1820s America, but not as a guide to identity, not as the system of networking. Instead people knew each other and related to each other through political parties or, sometimes, societies like the Masons. Mostly, though, the fundamental connections were between employee and employer, where the person hiring was of higher status, or between client and professional, where the person being hired had the higher status (as with doctors and lawyers).

So where are those trade relationships in the Book of Mormon? All of Joseph Smith's youth was spent working for hire for one farmer or another. But the one place in the Book of Mormon where one man goes to work for another as an employee is when Ammon goes to work for King Lamoni, and there is nothing in that relationship that remotely resembles the pattern of hiring for pay that Joseph Smith knew. Lawyers are also paid, but we don't see them hanging out their shingle and taking all comers. And that's it, as far as trade is concerned. The pattern of relationships outside the family that Joseph Smith knew best simply isn't echoed in the Book of Mormon.

In Mesoamerica, of course, there was no such thing as hiring tradesmen. Everybody did everything. When it was time to work in the fields, all the people of the working class did field work. When it was time to build public works, all the people of the working class built public works. And in the meantime, the rulers supervised them, and the priests did their rituals and carried out their studies and observations and wrote their records. When people did specialize—as in engraving on stone or creating artworks—they did so only under royal order, and not as freelancers working for pay. There was no such thing as a middle class, or even a free working class. And this is the culture that best fits the pattern that we see in the Book of Mormon. When the Lamanites come to rule over the people of King Limhi, the king of the Lamanites does not assign them to any new tasks, but rather takes an oppressive percentage of their crops and sets guards to keep them in place. The conqueror of Alma's people was able to set taskmasters over them, though he does nothing to reorganize their society. Why? Because their pattern *already* was to work the fields together, so that they would pursue their normal labors. The only difference was that instead of having their own rulers lead them in the fields, they had Lamanite guards or taskmasters watching to make sure that they didn't slack off or steal or escape into the wilderness.

The common people of any Book of Mormon city seem to be able to be assembled at any time. When Alma wants to speak to the poor who are ruled by the Zoramites, he doesn't have to go house to house, or find them in their various jobs. They already work together; he has only to ask for their attention and address them. Yet Joseph Smith does nothing to point out how different Book of Mormon jobs and trades are from the ones he knew. Why? Because he was translating a document that was written by somebody who didn't think to point out these patterns for the good reason that he didn't know there *was* another way to organize labor. Again, the Book of Mormon acts like a genuine document from the culture it depicts, rather than a story written by someone making up a pseudo-alien culture.

Swooning. Where did Joseph Smith get this business of people swooning to show great feeling? Especially men! That was unthinkable in the 1820s. A man fainting and then lying as if dead for several days? That doesn't reflect any social patterns in Joseph Smith's culture. In fact, it's embarrassing, right? We resist fainting, we don't celebrate it. And yet Mesoamerican culture is quite comfortable with people responding to emotional stress with a swoon—especially a religious experience.

Kings and Sub-kings. And what's this bit about a king having a father—alive—who is also king? That makes perfect sense in Mayan culture, where a son of a king can be a king somewhere else. There are sub-kings all over the place. But the only system of kingship that Joseph Smith knew anything about was the European pattern, and in Europe if you have a son of a king who proclaims himself king, you end up with a civil war. So how did Joseph Smith, if he was creating a hoax, dare to depart so radically from any pattern of kingship that anybody had ever heard of? And in doing so, how did he happen to get it dead right for Mesoamerican culture?

Writing Matters

Why do these elements escape the notice of most critics? Because the text doesn't emphasize them in any way. You only get them by implication. There are, of course, those who argue that because they're only found by implication, they're not there at all, but I think that when you compare them with documents from other alien cultures, you can see that these cultural differences are definitely real. All that's missing is the stuff that should have been there if Joseph Smith made it up.

Authorial Interests. The Book of Mormon never explains a lot of things that we wish it would. No one ever tells us in any great detail, for instance, what the people eat and drink. We are told that the rich have fine clothing, but no one describes what they actually wear. While the people seem to work collectively, we are never told exactly what their daily work is. Why? None of that is relevant to the historian or his purpose.

The Book of Mormon never loses track of the rhetorical purpose of the author—but also changes the rhetorical purpose with each author. Nephi and Jacob are not writing for the same reason as Mormon and Moroni, and therefore they include different kinds of information. Nephi glides over battles without detail; Mormon gives us detailed campaigns, but primarily when telling the story of a heroic captain who is a spiritual as well as a military example. And it's worth noting that the only captain whose battle strategies are given in detail is the very one that Mormon named his son after. It is arguable that Gidgiddoni's military achievements are at least equal to Moroni's—but we get no details of *his* campaigns.

Thus the Book of Mormon not only reflects the rhetorical purposes of the writers but also reflects their personal interests and concerns. They should be and are different from each other. Nobody else is as interested in military matters as Mormon, and nobody else writes about them. And, in fact, it is worth pointing out that nowhere else in all of Joseph Smith's writings do we get the slightest hint of *his* having an interest in military strategies or achievements. Even when he founded the Nauvoo Legion and dressed up in uniform, there is no evidence of his plotting military campaigns—yet if he were the author of those accounts of Moroni's and Helaman's campaigns, it is unthinkable that he would not have talked and thought about military matters, especially during those times in early Church history when such conversation and thought would have been appropriate. There were others in the Church who reveled in military matters—Sampson Avard, for instance. But Joseph Smith was not one of them. To me, that says that he could not have been the author of the book of Alma. I have read too much not to know that writers repeatedly return to whatever fascinates them. Just as Mormon brings up military matters again and again, though never with the same detail he brings to the campaigns of Moroni, we also find that Nephi and Moroni *never* bring up military matters with any detail at all. They are not interested and Joseph Smith was not interested, but Mormon *was* interested and his writings reflect that.

Exposition. When science fiction was just beginning, it was common for writers to stop the action in order to explain the cool new science or technology that they were introducing in the tale. It was not until Robert Heinlein that science fiction writers began to weave their exposition more subtly into the action of the story. The classic example is when, in telling of a character leaving a room, Heinlein wrote, "The door dilated." No explanation of the nifty technology behind dilating doors—just a simple statement that seems to take the new technology for granted.

This was a great step forward, allowing science fiction writers to introduce a vast amount of novelty into a story without stopping the forward movement of the plot in order to explain it. It required that readers adopt a new way of reading, however. Now, instead of the writer immediately telling the reader everything that is strange in the world of the story, the reader has to hold his sense of reality in abeyance, waiting and watching for each new bit of information that allows him to build up a picture of how the society differs from the here and now.

However, this more subtle kind of exposition is only practiced within the field of science fiction. Whenever mainstream writers who are not familiar with science fiction venture into the field—as with Margaret Atwood or Gore Vidal—they have no clue how to handle exposition. They go right back to stopping the action cold to explain things. And this is exactly what we should have expected the writer of the Book of Mormon to do.

It's worth pointing out, however, that handling exposition the way we science fiction writers do it is not correct, either, in documents that actually arise from the alien culture. It's easier and smoother to read, but it *still* points up the strangeness. Heinlein wrote "the door dilated" specifically because he knew his readers would not expect it to dilate and would recognize it as an item of future technology. But someone in that culture, writing about someone leaving a room, would rarely bother to mention the door at all. "He left" would do the job nicely, because there would be nothing unusual about the door to make it worth pointing it out. And if the writer claimed to be writing a shortened or abridged story, he would hardly waste his time on unnecessary explanations of things that didn't seem unusual in any way. So even the sophisticated method of science fiction exposition is not appropriate in the Book of Mormon, and in fact is not used there.

The remarkable thing in the Book of Mormon is that only once in the whole book does the author stop cold to explain something. Do you remember where that is? It has to do with the monetary system. In the middle of the account of Zeezrom, the lawyer, the action suddenly stops cold. Why? Because the value of money is surely something that would have changed across the 300 or 400 years between Zeezrom and Mormon. *That's* a cultural difference *Mormon* would recognize. And, predictably, like any naive writer, he stops the action in order to explain the unfamiliar facts. But notice how he does it. There is no absolute reference. Apparently one of those words or values in his list still meant something in the fourth century A.D. He didn't think to tell us exactly what you could *buy* with a senine, and certainly not in any terms that would mean anything to an 1820s reader, because Mormon must have considered the value of some element in the monetary system to be obvious. So even in the one place where we do get an "expository lump," it's handled exactly as a writer from the alien culture would have handled it, and utterly without reference to the 1820s.

Structure. The organization of the books in the Book of Mormon is peculiar in the extreme. Each of the books that Mormon wrote—Mosiah, Alma, Helaman, 3 Nephi—spends much of its time talking about someone other than the person the book was named for. The book of Mosiah starts with King Benjamin and then proceeds to tell us mostly about people such as King Noah, Abinadi, King Limhi, and the prophet Alma. Then the book of Alma turns out *not* to be about Alma the Elder but rather about Alma the Younger—and even at that, the latter part of the book focuses on his son Helaman. But the book of Helaman is *not* about Helaman the son of Alma. Rather it starts out with Helaman's son, Helaman, Jr.

And partway through the book of Helaman, we find that it is now about Helaman's son Nephi. But when we come to the book of 3 Nephi, it is not about *that* Nephi at all. Rather it is about his *son* Nephi.

What an odd pattern, don't you think? A book named for one man is as much about his son or successor. And when a book might be named for that son or successor, it turns out actually to be named for the successor's successor, who happens to have the same name. This pattern holds true even with the book named for Mormon himself—which was finished by his son, Moroni, who tells us later that he never expected to write a book that had his own name on it. He would have been content to have written the last part of the book named for his father.

I have no idea what this means. I simply point it out because it makes no sense in terms of Joseph Smith's culture, and it is hard to fathom why an American in the 1820s, whose only scriptural model was the Old and New Testaments, would structure his own work of scripture this way. The book of Ruth is about Ruth. The book of Isaiah includes the writings of Isaiah, and not a single story about Jonah or Ezekiel. The Gospels are named for their authors, but Mark doesn't pick up midway through the book of Matthew. If he were trying to create a hoax that would be accepted as scripture by 1820s Americans, why would Joseph Smith not simply pick one of the patterns in the Bible and follow it? Why would he come up with such a bizarre structure?

And then why did he throw in the Jaredites? I'm not even going to bother to explore the enormous complexity of Moroni's abridgment of Ether's abridgment of the Jaredite records. Hugh Nibley has a book on it that's better than anything that I could say. Suffice it to say that if you read *The World of the Jaredites* you'll realize that the book of Ether is rich in a culture that is strikingly different from the rest of the Book of Mormon—and from anything else that Joseph Smith would have any inkling of.

A Life-Changing Book

If you attempted to produce something like the Book of Mormon today, employing the best science fiction writers, fully aware of all that we know about the culture of Mesoamerica, fully aware of everything that we know about how you create a fake document, it would *still* be obvious—if not immediately, then within fifteen or twenty years. The cultural assumptions behind the book would reveal themselves, showing clearly when the book was really written. But the Book of Mormon has been around a lot longer than that, and believe me, folks, I really do understand a lot about how science fiction is made and I can't find anywhere that it's done wrong. Search all you like through that book. I have, and I can't find a flaw. Yet if the book were an 1820s fabrication we should expect to find a consistent pattern of getting it wrong. Not just one example but *thousands* of examples within a book that long. They are not there.

Now, does this mean that I've proved the Book of Mormon true? Obviously not. You can always still suppose that perhaps Joseph Smith or whoever wrote the Book of Mormon was the greatest and luckiest creator of phony documents from made-up alien cultures ever in history. The Book of Mormon only matters because it's a life-changing book.

The truth, the important truth of the Book of Mormon is *only* understood with the Spirit through faith. If you don't believe in the book, it's not going to change your life. And I mean believe in it in a way far different from believing it's a genuine artifact. You have to believe in it also as something meant for you as a guide to your life. So, I have very little interest in attempting to *prove* the book. I haven't proven it here. The only real proof is when you prove it with your life, living the gospel it teaches and participating in the Church that was established with that book as the mortar holding it all together.

But I do think it is important for us to look at this book, not *just* as wisdom literature, but also as a genuine artifact from another time. Those of us who already believe it must study this book as the product of a culture, as the product of the minds and hearts of the individual writers. When we do that, we will much better understand what it's for and what it means.

That's part of what I'm trying to do in my *Homecoming* books, examine the Book of Mormon, not as a scholar, because I'm not one, but as somebody whose business is making assumptions about the hearts and minds of individual human beings and telling stories about them that try to be as honest as possible. There are thousands of other ways to approach this book, of obtaining important, useful information from it, and I hope we'll use those ways, because if we treat it, as many Mormons do, as nothing more than a source of proof texts, we are missing the point and cheating ourselves of most of the value of this great work of scripture.

Joseph Smith didn't write the Book of Mormon, though he did translate it, so that his voice is present when we read it, including the flaws in his language and understanding. Those who wrote the original were also fallible human beings who will reveal their culture and their assumptions just as surely as the writers of "I Love Lucy" did. But unlike the writers of that TV show, the prophets wrote and translated under the direction of the Lord, out of love for us. It's well worth finding out who these men were, the culture from which they wrote, how it's different from ours, and how it's also very much the same.

Sunday Meetings: A Preparation for Work

From the *Ensign,* January 1978

It finally came home to him when a close friend died. "I had been meaning to visit Brian in the hospital," he said, "but I had to home teach on Tuesday night, and Wednesday I had a committee meeting. Thursday was my personal priesthood interview, and my wife had to leave right afterward to take her Beehives to the roller rink. And Friday night I spent writing my talk for sacrament meeting."

And then, on Saturday morning, the telephone call from Brian's son. "I know you and Dad were close," said the voice over the phone. "I thought you'd want to know."

"Want to know?" he said afterward. "I wanted more than to know. I wanted to turn back the clock, turn back the calendar, spend the few hours it would have taken to go to the hospital, talk over old times, remind my friend of my love for him, give him some comfort in the last pain and perhaps fear or loneliness before he died. But I was too busy."

The experience taught him something: "It's possible to be

so active in the Church that you forget to be active in the gospel."

But perhaps a better way to think about it is this: The meetings that we attend are for our preparation. Attending meetings should only be a small portion of our Church activity. Meetings are where we learn how to be active.

Gospel activity is just as much in our homes, among our friends, at work, in the community, among strangers, or alone in prayer, as it is in a meeting.

The Church provides many opportunities for activity: Home teachers and visiting teachers have splendid opportunities to serve others; teachers can uplift, inspire, and renew the faith of their students; quorum leaders can organize their brethren in good works.

But if we stop there, feeling satisfied that our attendance record means that we are sufficiently active, then in a sense we are like the servant who hid his talent in the earth. The Church provides us with a certain number of opportunities—but we have a responsibility to improve on that, to magnify those opportunities.

If all our good works are within the walls of the meetinghouse, then are we letting our light shine before men?

If we, like the Levite and the priest, are so intent on our Church business that we miss opportunities for charity to strangers, are we loving our neighbor as ourselves?

The Sabbath is the day the Lord has given us to rebuild, retrench, fortify our spirits and rest our bodies so that we can go out and live the gospel perfectly during the week.

"And though I have the gift of prophecy, and understand all mysteries, and all knowledge; and though I have all faith, so that I could remove mountains, and have not charity, I am nothing" (1 Corinthians 13:2).

A paraphrase: And though I attend all my meetings faithfully, and fulfill all my callings, and make a home teaching visit during the first week of the month; and though in all ways I am an active Church member, yet if I do not spend time in love and service for others, then I am not yet a Saint, for I do not yet love the Lord with *all* my heart, might, mind, and strength; and I do not love my neighbor as myself.

Let the Sabbath be a day for taking stock. (How active

have we been during the week in serving the Lord and his children?)

Let the Sabbath be a day for attending meetings, sharing with others our spirit, our understanding of how to serve the Lord.

And then let us use the other six days of each week as Christ did: in bringing joy to everyone we can. "I was an hungred," said the Lord, "and ye gave me meat: I was thirsty, and ye gave me drink: I was a stranger, and ye took me in: naked, and ye clothed me: I was sick, and ye visited me: I was in prison, and ye came unto me" (Matthew 25:35–36).

We are surrounded by those in need, both spiritually and physically. To be active in the Church, we must take the time from our busy schedules to fill those needs. For the gifts we offer to those around us we also offer to our Savior.

Family Art

From the *Ensign,* July 1977

When I was seven I drew constantly. Cars, trains, sailing ships. When I was through you could sometimes even tell what these things were supposed to be.

I did it for hours, sitting at the kitchen table, riding in the back of the old '55 Buick, or on a hard bench while making a valiant effort to be quiet in sacrament meeting.

No, I didn't plan to grow up to be a painter. My love for drawing had no purpose beyond the picture I was creating at the moment. It was *fun.*

That sense of fun children have in creating things is one of the greatest opportunities parents have: a chance to inspire, to teach, to learn, and to understand. By encouraging children in their natural creative activities, and by channeling those activities from time to time, parents can help their children learn vital principles and good personality traits—and the children will actually be teaching all this to themselves!

All the things that grown-up artists do, children do. They

don't have professional polish, but they do have a gusto that many professionals could well emulate. Children sing, making up their own lyrics and melodies. They dance, and though they don't quite have the stamina to step *en pointe,* they do love to move their bodies with people watching. They draw crazy circles and dots and lines and tell you that it is a picture of Mommy and Daddy—only a grown-up could possibly fail to recognize them. They playact with each other for hours on end. Sand becomes forts; dirt becomes highways for little cars; grass is a forest where giant insects lurk behind every blade.

Teenage artists are often better at their art than their parents are. Some of the best road shows ever produced have been written, directed, and acted by a cast and crew composed entirely of teenagers. Adolescence is a time when children become more serious than ever about their artistic efforts—and their attempts to draw, write, dance, sing, or act are closely linked to their search for identity. The poem your high school sophomore brings home from school may not be Shakespeare, but it's usually an honest effort to express himself. And some of those poems may be better than you expect: creative genius often manifests itself in early years.

The arts are in us, no matter what our age, and somehow we recognize that in them is one of our most effective ways of communicating with others—and of understanding ourselves. Not every child who builds with blocks is going to grow up to be an architect. But a child's plunges into art have long-lasting results that are sometimes more important to his adult happiness than a choice of career.

We must remember that children don't think their activities are childish, and adolescents often view themselves as adults: they attach as much importance to their arts as adults do.

Adults with the weight of the world on their shoulders find it too easy to forget that children do not know that their concerns are trivial. Imagine a man coming home from work, enthusiastic about the account he just landed with a million-dollar-a-year customer—how would he react if his wife patted his head and said, "How darling! What a cutey you are!"

To enter into children's lives, whatever their age, we must take their art as seriously as they do. To enhance our children's lives, we must provide them with opportunities to create and feel appreciated for what they have created. And, in the process, we can use their very seriousness to instill in them a love for righteousness and truth that will not leave them when they are adults.

People remember what they *do* far better than they remember what they see and hear. The story of Christmas may be loved when Daddy reads it from a book. But it becomes indelibly printed on their minds when little Roger is a shepherd and twelve-year-old Todd is Joseph and fourteen-year-old Agnes is Mary and they get to hold their own newborn brother as if he were the Christ child.

With a little channeling from parents, those marvelous small artists who decorate the walls of your home and bellow through your living room during Custer's millionth last stand can teach themselves in ways you never thought possible. And a lot of encouragement can help teenagers find creative outlets they may not have known they had—and which they can use to enrich the lives of their family. Take their art seriously, and their creations will become bonds that keep the family strong and close during adulthood.

Some ideas:

Drama. Children are natural actors, playwrights, directors. Domestic comedies are acted out in dollhouses and play kitchens. High drama accompanies the death of every cowboy and Indian in the back yard.

And if parents are willing to let the children take an active part, theatre at home can make the gospel come to life.

There are very few scriptural stories that can't be acted out. It can start in home evening after Daddy or Mommy tells the story of, let's say, Moses and the parting of the Red Sea.

"Who wants to be Moses?" Mommy asks, when the story is over.

"Me," say three or four small voices.

So Mommy picks one. *Not* necessarily the biggest—not necessarily a boy. Perhaps the eagerest.

Moses must be equipped with a robe and a staff, so the young actor is dispatched to the bedroom to find something he can use. In the meantime, Daddy falls to the floor and starts waving his arms and legs in the air.

"I'm the Red Sea," he says solemnly. When the children

laugh, Daddy tickles the nearest small foot and says, "Better watch it; I can be dangerous."

"Who wants to be the children of Israel? And who wants to be the Egyptians?" and in a few moments a small Egyptian army is gathered behind the lone Israelite. Mommy stands up. "I'm the pillar of fire," she announces. Moses comes back with his father's bathrobe and a fishing rod (a quick check follows to make sure there's no hook dangling from it), and the story begins.

With reminders from Mom, the children of Israel see the Egyptians coming (and they do look pretty fierce), but the Lord saves them by sending a pillar of fire. Then Moses raises his staff and Daddy's arms and legs move apart, leaving a channel across "dry land"—Daddy's stomach. The children of Israel step gingerly across, with Daddy grunting a little from the patter of tiny feet. When Moses has crossed, his staff held high the whole time, the pillar of fire moves aside, and the Egyptians begin to cross.

But when they reach the Red Sea, Moses lowers his staff, and all of a sudden the Egyptians are lost in a tumble of Daddy's limbs. (Chances are pretty good that at least one Egyptian gets through, and then Mommy has to explain that it didn't really happen that way, but the story will never be forgotten.)

As the children get older, the stories and the action can be a little more sophisticated. Laman and Lemuel must be sullen and unresponsive. Joseph Smith must be on fire with indignation as he rebukes the guards in Missouri. Ruth must be loving and Naomi is kind as she tries to turn her daughter-in-law away. Other emotions besides fun come into use.

Teenage children are usually more comfortable with a written script—so let them write one! For the week before a special home evening they may be laboring over memorizing the lines they have invented for Saul to say to David. Both the writing and the performing can be fun—as well as profound learning experiences. If memorizing is too much, let your children read the script: What matters is the fact of sharing and learning.

Scripture isn't the only source for drama. Is there a problem with quarreling among your children? Why not assign one of your teenagers to write a small play about a family that has such a problem? And if there is a special event in your family, why not a play to commemorate it? (Special events can be anything from a trip to a national park or the onset of spring to a son leaving on a mission or a healing by the power of the priesthood.)

If no one has a writing bent, there is still a lot your teenagers can do with drama. A great modern play like *A Man for All Seasons* or *The Diary of Anne Frank* can be read aloud, with family members each taking a part—or several parts. Though none of your family may be Academy Award material, the great characters of theatre and their heroic struggles mean far more if you have said their words and done their deeds yourself.

And then you can try theatre without writing at all. A lot can be learned by improvised role-playing. Just select the issue or subject and let them play it out. What about having two of your teenagers play the role of parents, while you take the child roles? Chances are you'll have a golden opportunity to see yourself as they see you—and vice versa.

And sometimes you may want to have a family play with all the trappings—sets, costumes, lights, even an audience. Perhaps your family could do a pageant of family history for the annual family reunion. Or a scriptural play for each other.

There's no law that says you have to have an audience for drama to be meaningful to your family. One of the most satisfying and powerful experiences I've ever had with theatre was without an audience. My younger brother and I were rehearsing for a community theatre production. I was playing his father, and in one highly emotional scene the character I was playing did something that hurt him deeply. Tears came into his eyes, and, even though we were acting, the thought that I had caused him sorrow filled me also with grief, and for a moment I stepped outside of the play and saw Russell for what he is—one of the most important people in my life—and I remembered what humdrum family life often causes me to ignore: that I love my family better than I love myself.

I didn't need an audience, just my brother and me reading lines from a play; and yet the scene and the characters we were playing helped us transcend the ordinary and touch each other deeply. That moment was never equaled, even when we performed the play in front of audiences.

Music. In the old days, hymns used to be sung to only a few well-known melodies. Even some Latter-day Saint hymns were written to old tunes. There's no reason why you can't make up new lyrics to songs your children already know. Or, better, have the older children and teenagers make up the new lyrics themselves. Perhaps a particular point needs to be stressed in an upcoming family home evening—you could hand a hymnbook to one of your teenagers and tell him or her the topic you want stressed. Then the whole family can learn the new hymn the next week.

And family home evening is not the only opportunity: Why not gather around the piano (organ, autoharp, guitar, recorder) on Sunday before or after meetings and sing hymns and old favorite songs?

Many mothers make up spur-of-the-moment songs with never-before-heard melodies. Somehow anger gets sidetracked if mother *sings,* "If you leave your toys out in the living room, my dears, I don't think I will serve you any supper." It becomes funny and fun instead of a dire threat—but the point gets made. And music can just flow from the joy of the moment: "I love all my children, especially you while you're smiling at me as I cook up your dinner," sings a mother to a five-year-old. Will the child forget?

Little children are great spur-of-the-moment singers, too. "Can you sing a song about how you love your brother Michael?" two-year-old Tricia is asked. "I love my brother Michael," she sings, "because he is a good baby. He cries a lot but he is still nice and I like to hug him and kiss him." Then a kiss, and she starts singing about graham crackers and the lesson is over, but she has learned to speak her love aloud, and to let her emotions overflow in song.

Singing isn't restricted to mothers and little children, either. Heavy yard work feels lighter with Father and sons singing the Volga Boat Song as they work. "Yo Heave Ho! Yo Heave Ho!" can make the worst drudgery fun. And what about "Put Your Shoulder to the Wheel," "Whistle While You Work," and even "When We're Helping We're Happy"?

There is something powerful in songs that belong only to you. Why else do hymns like "We Thank Thee, O God, for a Prophet" and "Come, Come, Ye Saints" make Mormons feel such a bond? If your family develops Christmas carols that only you know, or has special songs about going to the temple or on a mission someday that no one outside your family has ever heard, those songs become ties that bind you closer. They'll never be forgotten.

Dance. For those of us who are not agile, dance seems well beyond reach. But most children are agile to the point of contortionism (remember when you were three and could do a backbend and touch your feet to the back of your head?), and dance is as natural to them as breathing.

Dance can follow lesson themes where younger children might not be able to follow complicated story lines. "Dance sad," the little ones might be told, "because that's how the Nephites felt when they disobeyed the Lord." Sad music on the record player helps set the mood. After a short time, the music is changed. "Now they have repented," the children are told, "so dance happy, the way the Nephites felt when they obeyed."

Dance isn't just restricted to the little children, however. Most homes aren't big enough for dancing indoors—but there's always the back yard in the summer. Why not have a square dance on the lawn for the teenagers? Or plunge back into the family heritage: find someone to come and teach you a Danish (English, Scottish, Japanese, Mexican) folk dance as a family activity; it helps make our ties to the "old country" and our ancestors who were born there become real to us in our modern cities.

Dance can become a game, too. Did your great-grandfather live on a farm? Have everybody in the family, young and old, think of a farm activity and then act it out without words (sometimes it's better not to tell self-conscious teenagers that what they're doing is really dancing). Everybody guesses what each action is, and then when all have chosen one, you can do them at once, and then trade around a circle until everyone has "experienced" farm life. Or life on shipboard sailing to New England or Australia or from Jutland to Kent. Or crossing the plains. Or building the temple. Disguised as a game, dance can be a great teacher—and a great source of fun.

A side effect of keeping dance alive through family activities is that you may be able to avoid the tendency among modern adults to not express themselves physically. If your children grow up expressing themselves with their bodies, they will never become stiff, awkward, closed-off adults who treat their bodies like temporary equipment instead of feeling at home with their own arms and legs.

Drawing. This is one of the easiest arts to get children of any age to do—as any parent whose squirmy child has quieted down with a pencil and paper can tell you. But like the other arts, this has many uses other than just getting a respite from the wrigglers. Drawing can be a game: One family member is the artist. "We're drawing a car," he says. "First draw the wheels." Everyone does, then passes the sheet of paper to the left. On the new sheet, which already has four wheels, everyone adds what the artist directs: "Now draw the body of the car."

"Now the windows and doors."

"Now the people."

"Now the scenery."

As your children get older, it will no longer be a challenge to make something that looks like a car. Then the fun comes from visual jokes and playfulness: when the artist says to draw any water that might be in the scene, someone puts in water faucets and people boating in large kitchen sinks.

A variation is "draw the monster," dreaming up the wildest possible creatures and applauding the ones that by chance turn out the best.

Coloring and painting can be messy, but they last. If the children are young and their drawings are too "modern" for you, make a note of what they said the drawing was supposed to be, and then from time to time you can point to where it's hanging on the refrigerator door and say, "Remember when you drew that picture of the angel telling Mary about Christ's birth? Tell me the story."

The story you hear may not be the story you told, but you'll probably be amazed at how much the child remembers.

And adolescents who draw recognizably—even well—can be assigned to illustrate a particular story for an upcoming home evening lesson. Then, as you tell the story, you can bet at least *one* pair of eyes will be riveted on those drawings. And the other children, too, will be excited that one of their brothers or sisters has done what so often is left up to the manual. The art print of Jesus in Gethsemane may be more attractive to your adult eye, but the drawing your own child makes will get a lot more attention from his.

One family even does their own "editorial" cartoons, depicting some aspect of family life they're working on improving or some special event they're commemorating. When the cartoons come off the wall they go straight into the family history, never to be lost or forgotten.

And art doesn't have to be small. Butcher paper in the family room can become a mural about family history, Church history, scripture, contemporary family life—anything. And then there are the big signs on garage doors or front windows saying, "Welcome home, Jimmy," to a returning missionary or serviceman.

The Lloyd Wilson family in Pacifica, California, goes crazy over decorations—every holiday is an excuse. The parents set a few rules (to keep the house intact), and then the eleven children are free to dangle decorations throughout the living room. Halloween, Christmas, Thanksgiving, winter, spring, Easter, Presidents' Day, the Fourth of July and Twenty-fourth of July—who needs an excuse? The living room blossoms and so do the children's smiles.

Art is for the parents, too. Last Christmas my father did his first serious painting in twenty-five years—the first I had ever seen him do. He gave it to my mother for Christmas, a scene that had what my mother always wanted in a painting: mountains, water, sky, and autumn colors. I know that I've never seen another gift that meant so much to my mother. And it meant a lot to us kids too—Mom wasn't the only one who cried. I am sure that painting will stay in the family for generations, always prized more than any painting we could buy.

Building. Talking about the temple at Jerusalem in family home evening? You can have a miniature temple ready-built out of plastic bricks or wooden blocks. In fact, you'll find it hard to stop your children from building. How many slabs of wood do children nail together, hoping their "boat" will float? That boat can also teach, as you point out how it is like the one that almost sank until Christ stilled the waves.

That much-dug dirt pile in the backyard can become the earthen walls that Moroni built around the city of Bountiful.

Family building projects can also beautify the home. Saving money isn't the *only* reason why you might want your teenagers to help you build the fence around your yard. Curtains, dish towels, rugs, plant hangers—bought in a store they might look more professional, but made at home by your growing-up children they'll turn your house into a home your children will love in memory forever.

One engaged couple put together a "personal history" montage in a wooden box. Squares within the box displayed political campaign buttons, Bicentennial medallions, baby pictures, small toys, and a current picture with swatches of the fabric from the wedding dress. They photographed it and printed the photograph on their wedding invitations. Similar boxes can display items of interest to the whole family—and perhaps an annual collection of things to remind you of the year's events could become part of your family history. Children of any age can take part in this kind of project, and people without children at home can enjoy it, too.

Other home crafts become part of your tradition as well. Macrame, embroidery, tatting, knitting, crocheting, quilting, weaving, and sewing all create keepsakes and family heirlooms that will someday serve to tie the generations together.

Writing. Children learn to love reading because of the stories their parents tell them. Though picture books are delightful ways to trigger children's imaginations, children often prefer the "tailor-made" stories their parents tell. Stories about a child with your little one's name who gets into all kinds of adventures that he or she can identify with will always hold interest, and as the story-child learns honesty and faith and kindness, so will the real one who is eagerly listening.

Children also tell each other far wilder and more creative stories than parents would dare to dream up, and the teller profits as much as the listeners. Great things can happen to family unity when the older children sometimes put the younger ones to bed with a story or a song. Bonds can be made at bedtime that will never break—all through the children's sharing the art of storytelling with each other.

Does your fourth-grader write haikus for school? Ask him to write a haiku about spring for a family home evening, and then let that lead you into a discussion of the Lord's work of creation. And not just the fourth-grader—Grandfather's doggerel can delight the family for years.

The old "story game" is a great way to keep storytelling ability alive in your family. One person starts a story and puts the hero or heroine in some perilous position—and stops. The next person must take over, extricate the character, and go on. Ghost stories are scarier and yet much more fun with this approach, and the wilder the adventures the better. The story you end up with may not have much relation to the one you started, but who cares?

Writing can be the key to your family history. My family, with children all over twelve, is trying an experiment with writing memories. We have a list of topics that will cue our memories—like "houses we've lived in" and "Delpha's childhood" and "spiritual experiences." Every day or so we pull out notebooks, when we have (or make) the time, and write for fifteen minutes or a half hour, rip out the sheet, and put it in a file folder labeled with the category. After a few months, we'll have enough memories to start our family history, and as more memories occur to us over the years, it is infinitely expandable.

Another idea, which can apply to families with children of all ages, is to spend a family home evening making a "family book." First, everyone is given a sheet of paper the same size. All write down a true story—or a fictional one—on a similar topic: a time when someone was nice to me; why I try to be honest; why I love Johnny. The littlest ones draw a picture or tell a story to Mom or Dad. Then the pages are collected and bound into a book with cardboard or wooden covers that anyone can look at and remember. The book can be illustrated, too, and the binding itself can be a family activity.

Older children and teenagers can be assigned to write essays on scriptural themes, historical events, recent family happenings, or practically anything else, and then read them to the family. They might even discover that reports can be fun—when no one is grading them or correcting their grammar, and all they have to do is say what they think.

Family letters to members who are gone—at college, on missions, in the service, married and moved away—are good uses of writing skills. And we're all encouraged to keep journals: why not devote a half hour on Sunday to making journal entries, with a chance to share items of general interest, though private, personal writing could be kept secret.

Best of all, practice at writing and storytelling within the uncritical family circle can instill a love for writing in your children. It can also sharpen their skills through practice, and help them be better able to express themselves verbally in adulthood.

Why art at home?

Why not? It comes naturally to little children, and teenagers have it at their fingertips. We only lose it through the process of growing up into set molds. By keeping many opportunities around for your family to express themselves in drama, music, dance, drawing, building, and writing, you encourage them to keep the creativity they brought with them to this world.

But even more important, the arts are also great opportunities for young people to teach themselves principles of the gospel. Through family art activities, traditions are created that bind the family together as closely as families should be tied. And even though most children are not going to pursue a career in the arts, the background in self-expression will help them be happy, well-adjusted, self-confident people who can cope with the ups and downs of living in the adult world.

And besides the art that your children create themselves, they can also learn to understand and love the art created by the masters. Trips to art shows, movies, plays, dance productions; excursions to look at beautiful buildings and homes; good books read as families and given to children to read alone—all of them mean more when the children have tried creating such things themselves. At the same time, exposure to the work of the masters helps them learn the meaning of excellence, helps them understand the difference between beauty and ugliness. A home where great classical music and wholesome contemporary music are heard at least as often as television theme songs, where fine books are on the table beside *Reader's Digest* and *TV Guide,* will produce young people with taste and discernment, who love what is good and beautiful because they have grown up with it all their lives.

And even if you, as parents, feel lacking in talent or experience with the arts, that shouldn't stop you from trying. Your children won't know that you sing off-key or that you're borrowing the plots for your stories from *Grimm's Fairy Tales*—and as they grow and develop in their abilities, so will you, enjoying it all the while.

The family is the only really uncritical, accepting audience most of us will ever have. Why not open ourselves and let the arts have a place in our homes? Married or not, young or old, with young children or teenagers, through the arts we can give those we love a part of ourselves. You can't put a price on it, and no assembly line can turn out a good substitute. Families need each other, and through family art—especially with a gospel orientation—we can help satisfy each other's needs.

PART TWO

Moral Storytelling

There is no society that does not have some kind of fiction, and there's a reason for that. "True" stories are always subject to revision. We may think we know why something happened, but there's always a possibility of new evidence or a new interpretation. The event really happened, but *why* it happened can never be known for sure. In fiction, however, precisely *because* the characters and events are all made up, causality can never be called into question. If the author says that a character did something for a certain reason, that reason can never be called into question except by the author himself, somewhere else in the text. Thus, while the event never really happened, *why* it happened can be known with absolute certainty. We need that kind of sureness in our lives. It is one of the prime functions of art that, at the cost of placing artificial limits on reality, it offers us meaning.

But what meaning does it offer? I believe firmly that art not only is *good* or *bad,* in the sense of being well or badly made, but also is *good* or *evil,* in the sense of making real people better or worse off for having experienced the art.

The older I get, the less tolerance I have for tragedy in art. As a teenager and in my unmarried twenties, I thrived on Romance, on noble suffering, the stuff of great myths. But as my wife and I had children and watched them grow, there was enough real fear and worry in our lives that I began to want to spend more of my time watching comedies than tragedies; I began to shun stories that would make me experience sorrow (though I still watched them, when they looked as though the suffering would mean something). I think this transformation is a common one, and can be explained simply enough: As an adolescent I had no responsibility for anyone beyond myself, and therefore needed tragic stories in order to give me a sense of meaning and importance in my life. As an adult, with serious responsibilities for the life and well-being of others, I had enough real dread, enough genuine problems that what I needed was encouragement. Meaning I had enough of at the time.

My point is that at different times we look for different things in art, and the same thing is true of the artist. What we don't do is lose the need for art, particularly for storytelling. Those who claim they never read a book or watch TV are nevertheless getting their stories somewhere—if from nowhere else, then from gossip, the great universal storytelling machine. And just as gossip focuses on the unpleasant or the shocking, so also fiction and all other forms of storytelling bring us experiences that we would usually rather not go through in person. Even comedies depend utterly on the characters' pain; they become comedies only because of the exaggerated response of the characters—and because we can be assured of a happy (or happy-ish) ending. But in comedy or tragedy alike, if the pain becomes too great for an audience member, he rebels and rejects the story. Thus I have met people who found the brilliant comedy *A Fish Called Wanda* too painful to be funny, though I loved every moment of it; at the same time, I have found myself so vicariously embarrassed by the pathetic self-humiliation of Kirstie Alley's character on "Cheers" that I had to leave the room or change channels, even though I recognized that her performance was excellent and the comedy true to life. I have a threshold for endurable pain, and when art crosses that threshold, I can't endure it. Other people also have such a threshold, and I am quite aware that I, as a storyteller, will inevitably cross that threshold for someone with everything I write.

In other words, for one reason or another, someone is going to be offended by everything I write. The only story that doesn't offend *somebody* is the one that nobody sees. Every bishop of every ward has run into the same problem: There is no decision he can make, no calling he can issue, that won't cause *somebody* to get upset. But you just have to go on doing your best, trusting that others will forgive you for your mistakes because of their trust that you are doing your best.

Unfortunately, some people thrive on the assumption that others are *not* doing their best. And, in fact, some storytellers—and some bishops—really *are* blowing it, making the wrong decisions for the wrong reasons, causing avoidable harm. It happens, and it is a foolish person indeed who denies it.

Some storytelling is good, and some is evil. Some decisions artists make are right, and some are wrong, not just in an artistic sense, but in a moral one as well. It is worth exploring the right and wrong in art, and the next two pieces do exactly that. Inevitably, because I am a practitioner of the storytelling art, my ponderings, however abstract they might seem, are intensely personal. But I try to be as unsparing of myself and my fellow artists as I can manage.

The Problem of Evil in Fiction

A speech given at BYU for its Church sesquicentennial lecture series on Mormon arts, letters, and sciences, March 1980

In January 1977, at a time when I worked as an assistant editor at the *Ensign*, we ran an article designed to encourage inactive Latter-day Saints to prepare themselves to seal their marriages in the temple. It was a struggle to come up with an eye-catching photograph to lead off the article, but what we decided to do was show an inactive father reading that very article, so that he held a picture of himself holding a picture of himself holding a picture of himself. The only problem was how to show that he was inactive. Since we at the *Ensign* had not yet earned any fame for our subtlety, we decided on the most obvious symbol—right in the dead center of the picture was an unlighted pipe sitting in an ashtray. If that didn't suggest an inactive Mormon, we would despair of our audience's power of reasoning.

Alas, we had underestimated the ability of some people to misunderstand. A certain small percentage of our readership wrote letters protesting that illustration. They fell into three categories:

1. "Aha! You thought you could put one over on us, didn't you, running that picture of a pipe in the *Ensign,* but we caught you!"

2. "We thought there was one place that we could count on never to show evil, but there it was, right where our children could see it, an actual pipe, and in the *Ensign,* no less, our modern-day scripture!"

3. "Don't you people check this stuff before you print it? Right there in the middle of a picture on page 60, there was a pipe! You really ought to screen your pictures more carefully, if mistakes like that are getting through!"

These few letter-writers had got part of our message—they noticed the pipe, and they knew that for a Latter-day Saint, pipe smoking is evil. What they completely missed was our purpose in showing that evil—to attract the attention of people who might have that problem so we could help them solve it.

Showing evil is not necessarily advocating it.

The Worst Things in Life Are Essential

The question of whether and how evil ought to be presented in art is one that intrigues a lot of people. Some people regard it as their life's work to drive pornography, the ultimate artistic expression of evil, completely out of their community. Others regard it as their life's work to use their talents to explore and understand evil in their art. I am a two-headed animal; born and raised in an orthodox Mormon family, I couldn't escape the Latter-day Saint view of good and evil if I tried. And I don't try—I am a radically orthodox Mormon today, and have no intention of changing my beliefs on the subject. But as a writer of fiction, I have found it impossible to write well without dealing directly with evil, portraying it in my work.

Over the years, some people whose judgment I respect have asked me a question that you might think is naive, but it is not. "Why do you have to write such depressing stuff? Why can't you show the good things in life? Why do all your characters have to suffer?"

Well, why indeed? After all, fiction *isn't* fact. Fiction is *lies.* Those people are made up. They'd better be—if they're not, you can get sued. So as long as I'm making things up, why not make up a happy life for them?

The most obvious answer is also the most trivial: He who writes about happy people being happy in a happy world ain't gonna last long as a writer. Nobody cares about that happy stuff. Evil is intrinsically more interesting. More entertaining. Evil *sells.*

"Indeed," answers the English Puritan after Cromwell's successful revolution. "All these people are going to the theatre to see *evil* reenacted on the stage. We will make England a much better place if we simply ban theatre altogether. No more Macbeth and his bloody crimes. No more King Lear and his self-destructive madness. We have made the world safe for Christianity."

But it took about twenty minutes after the Puritans were thrown out for the theatre to be back in business. The people wanted it. And I don't think they wanted it because they were evil.

Evil is more entertaining than unrelenting goodness because any depiction of life without evil is a lie. Now, fiction *is* made up, but it is not all lies. Or rather, out of the sum of his lies the author's view of truth inevitably emerges, and if the writer has wrought skillfully, some portion of his view of the world will remain with the reader, changing and shaping him. While readers of fiction know perfectly well that what they're reading is made up, they also insist on the illusion of truth and on truth itself. First, the illusion of truth, because while the reader surrenders himself to the writer's controlled tour of the life experiences of some interesting characters, the reader insists on some correspondence between the surface details of the story and the reality that the reader knows in his own life. It must ring true. And second, the substance of truth, because no matter how many deliberate lies a writer tells, his own most deeply held beliefs about good and evil will inevitably appear in his work. It is impossible to write a morally neutral work of fiction.

Both the illusion of truth and the unavoidable substance of truth require evil to be present in fiction. Almost from the first moments of consciousness, human beings are aware of the fact that the world isn't always nice. My son Geoffrey, almost two, has had to face the bitter truth that his shoes won't always go on right. He has wept over the agonizing discovery that when he deliberately rubs jello in his hair, his lunch abruptly ends. Two nights ago, no matter how much he cried, Daddy and Mommy didn't make the thunder go away. And, the cruelest truth of all, the other children in the Primary class occasionally hit him and knock him down for no reason at all.

The painful lessons are only beginning. As we grow older, we learn that people die, even when we love them very much. Friends that we counted on cheat us. Family members that we love hurt us. People we never harmed commit crimes against us.

But we aren't always victims. It's sometimes a terrible discovery that we ourselves are the perpetrators of evil, but it's one we all make at some time or another. The world is often ugly, and uglier still is the realization that in our own small way we have darkened it for others, and for ourselves.

Nature, other people, and our own desires conspire to bring sorrow into our lives. No one is immune to that. No one is so good that he is untouched by evil.

And if that is life, how can a fiction writer honestly write without depicting evil in the lives of his characters?

The illusion of truth demands that there be evil, or his readers will cease believing in his characters and toss the book away.

And his own inner demand for the substance of truth requires that there be evil, because what in the world can a writer say about a character if he does not tell about the character's struggles against suffering? If the writer knew a way for a human being to live without evil, without suffering, without sorrow, he would go and live that way, and forget writing. But the writer—no, let's forget the third person—*I* know of no way to live untouched by evil, and so the characters that I write about will also confront evil. It is impossible to write any other way.

Of course, the Puritans of Cromwell's stripe in England had the answer to that. If you can't write any other way, then stop writing. If writers are only going to add to the total amount of evil in the world, then let's stop them from writing, for everyone's sake!

It can't be done. It's been tried. The Communist rulers of

the USSR kept it up for years. But even in the darkest times, there were those who would risk their lives in order to read good fiction and pass it on. In the samizdat system in Russia, the writer created his pack of truthful lies, and passed it to a friend, who could destroy him by giving the manuscript to the authorities. But instead the friend read it and laboriously typed his own copy—no xerox machines involved here—and then gave both copies to other friends. They could have been caught. They could have been imprisoned, torn from their loved ones for decades of slave labor; they could have been tortured; they could have been killed. But they read, they typed, they passed it on.

Of course, not many people took part in this. Even here in the United States, the overwhelming majority of us don't read a thing, if we can help it. The biggest bestsellers, the ones that take the reading public by storm, have never sold more than ten million copies. Out of a population of 220 million, that's a pathetically small 4.5 percent. And those are the bestsellers. My most recent paperback novel sold only forty thousand copies or so, and that's perfectly normal, better than average, in fact. My most recent hardback novel has sold only two thousand copies. Think of it—all that work, all that emotional involvement, and only one-thousandth of one percent of the American population has read it. In a nation of voluntary illiterates, who needs censorship?

Nevertheless, even in America there are those who would rather read than eat. Whatever it is they get from fiction, they need it.

And even those writers who can't find publishers for their work insist on writing manuscripts that are never read except by underpaid and uninsightful slush-pile readers, who tuck a rejection slip under the rubber band after reading twenty pages and send the manuscript back.

The need for fiction of some kind is almost universal. In preliterate societies, the storytellers are respected and loved; much of our scripture is devoted to recounting tales of evil people and righteous people in conflict; we sing about it, we dance about it, we perform plays about it, we make films about it. Even the silliest television series meet some of those same needs: on its most basic level, isn't "Laverne and Shirley" really about the struggle of the mentally deficient to find happiness in an unfriendly world?

Reality Is Just an Escapist Retreat from Fiction

You've all heard of escapist fiction, I'm sure. It's a myth, and one with little foundation in fact. The standard image is of a twenty-three-year-old housewife, three small children biting at her ankles, ironing with one hand as with the other hand she holds in front of her face a paperback book. On the cover is a picture of a girl about her age, running from a dark and sinister building that has one lighted window, as the sky looms and threatens a storm—and worse. Of course, say the believers in the stereotype. She's escaping from her humdrum life into a much more interesting fictional existence.

Escaping? I think not. Do you know what goes on in those gothic novels? If you actually identify with the main character, something that I am only occasionally capable of doing, you are put through terrible tension, an ordeal of fear and uncertainty, mistrust, pain, betrayal. The inevitably happy ending comes as a blessed relief, because along the way the poor reader has been through a grueling experience.

Science fiction is also branded as escapist. Anyone who believes such nonsense was simply incapable of identifying with Paul Muad'dib in *Dune,* as the beleaguered heir to an incredibly valuable world discovers a terrible destiny that he cannot avoid no matter how hard he tries. There is nothing escapist about Westerns or Harlequin romances or mysteries—not to readers who care about the characters. To me, the grim-faced, handsome cowboy who rides off into the sunset after curing all the town's ills is laughably unbelievable. But I can't dismiss the whole genre as escapist, not worthy of my consideration. I can only conclude that I am not a member of the audience for that particular sort of fiction. Because those who regularly buy and read those Westerns *do* care about that grim-faced, handsome cowboy. His experiences are their experiences. His fear is their fear. His pain is their pain. And, ultimately, his victory is their victory.

The appeal of fiction and, ultimately, of all the tale-telling arts, is catharsis. The character becomes the surrogate of the audience. The artist shapes the audience's experience, but ultimately the audience lives through the experience privately, personally, and emotionally. No matter how many millions of people sit in front of their televisions, no matter how many hundreds come to watch the play, each person is receiving an intimate, individual experience. It is never entirely the experience the writer created. It is always the experience of the character combined with the experience of the audience member.

That is why some works appeal more to some people than to others. I just gave a copy of my favorite novel of 1979, *Engine Summer* by John Crowley, to a friend of mine whose taste I respect. He hated it, thought it was the most boring thing he'd ever suffered through, and he was grateful that it was short. Yet to me, it was one of the most perfect books I have ever read, and it has already become a part of my life, part of the well of memory that I dip into constantly to replenish myself and to gather whatever wisdom I can find to make my decisions. Why did he receive it one way, and I another? Because we are different people, that's all, and a character I could identify with left him completely cold; writing that helped me into the story was a barrier to him.

Fiction is not an escape from reality. Fiction is simply another kind of reality, one which takes place within finite borders, between endpapers. Unlike life, it begins and ends; we can close the book and draw conclusions. It is often easier to learn from fiction than from life; but fiction is a necessity to so many of us because through it we live many lives, and learn many things, instead of staying in the much safer reality and learning only a few things.

Yet all of this depends on the reader's willingness and ability to add himself to the novel or the story. The illusion of reality must be built up within the reader's own mind. And those readers who lack the desire or the ability to join in the creative act *cannot* receive what the author is trying to give. That ability to share in the author's creation is one that develops through practice. Teachers of literature see it time after time. Young people weaned on Nancy Drew, an unusually simple kind of fiction, gradually learn to handle the better mystery writers, from simple works like those of Agatha Christie to more complex writers like Ross Macdonald and John le Carré. Suddenly they make the incredible leap to even more difficult writers like John Updike and John Fowles, and from there they spring joyously into the really great writings. Then, somewhere along there, they happen to pick up a copy of *The Hidden Staircase* (I mention that one because it was my favorite Nancy Drew when I was eight) or some other volume of Carolyn Keene's distinguished oeuvre, and they start to read. The stuff is trash! It's unreadable! By the second chapter you want to strangle Ned Nickerson! By page 60 you hope Nancy Drew falls in a mud puddle, or at least gets her hair mussed. And by the end you are either giggling uncontrollably or tearing the pages out one by one and ritually immolating them.

But the writing hasn't really got worse. The reader has simply got better. It takes years of mind-stretching reading to be able to receive the best fiction. An untrained or unpracticed reader is usually incapable of understanding what's going on. He finds it boring, affected, hoity-toity. And don't think the writers don't know the difference. Mario Puzo wrote a couple of decent, critically praised novels that sold seven copies each (I exaggerate, of course). He decided that this was ridiculous; he had a family to support. So he wrote a deliberate piece of trash called *The Godfather*. It made history—because it was accessible to a much larger audience that simply lacked the training and desire to read his more difficult but better works. I have a faint suspicion that John Irving's novel *The World According to Garp* was that little bit of history repeating itself, only more self-consciously and with a bit more style. (And I happen to think both books are better than the authors' more "serious" works.)

The point is that those who do not read are generally incapable of understanding what is going on in those few books that they attempt to read. Even those who *do* read are often unable to receive particular books that simply don't satisfy their personal needs and desires. Reading is individual. There is no universal standard for judging the worth of a piece of fiction.

Which Evil Is Good Evil?

Which finally brings us full circle—back to those people who misunderstood that pipe that appeared in the pages of the

Ensign magazine. They were able to recognize a pipe, and they knew that pipes were not good things for Mormons. What they seemed incapable of understanding was *why the pipe was there.*

We run into the same problem in dealing with evil in fiction. A lot of people who are alerted to the problems of pornography go to the bookstore, pick up a book they have heard about, or one with a particularly lurid cover, and start to read. They are perfectly able to understand what words the letters spell out. They can tell when a writer is talking about sex or violence or when some little four-letter clumps spell out words they'd wallop their kids for saying out loud. But, like those few readers of the *Ensign* who didn't understand the moral message behind the photograph of a pipe, they are simply incapable of understanding what is really going on in the fiction. They do not know how to tell the difference between an evil book and a good book that depicts evil. And since all fiction inevitably depicts evil somewhere, the well-meaning but functionally illiterate censor finds, to his horror, that every book he reads is just dreadfully bad, and should be banned.

That's why some of our modern self-appointed censors commit such absurdities as recommending that only *Tom Sawyer,* of all Mark Twain's works, be allowed in the public schools, and then only with certain strict warnings. Ban *The Prince and the Pauper*? Do you have any idea what goes *on* in that book? Why, there are criminals in there who blame their suffering on the system, and the book teaches children to feel sympathy for those who are justly punished for their crimes! And what about *Huckleberry Finn*? If that isn't a tract for rebelling against society, I don't know what is! Not to mention that ugly *n*-word on almost every page . . .

I can't think of a book you can't do that sort of thing to, if you are determined to misread and misunderstand the overall purpose of the book. I know of a book that shows two brothers who take over their parents' seagoing ship, tie up their younger brother and threaten to kill him, terrorize everyone aboard, and have a drunken orgy until the ship is almost destroyed. In that same book women and children are thrown into a fire alive; in a bloody little battle one of the good guys cuts off the scalp of his enemy and we're supposed to cheer; a woman arouses the lust of a man with her obscene dancing and gets him to kill the king. And if that isn't enough, another work by the same author gets heavily into human sacrifice and has a man who sets up a mafia-like organization in order to kill people without getting punished. Practically a blueprint for evil.

Just so that nobody here goes out trying to ban those books, I'll mention to the people who have been out to lunch for the last two years at BYU that the books I have just described are the Book of Mormon and the Pearl of Great Price.

Am I saying that *no* books are evil? That freedom of the press and freedom of speech should protect everything?

No. I'm saying that there is evil and there is evil—if you'll forgive the semantic absurdity, there is good evil and bad evil. And middling evil.

As a writer given to splitting infinitives, I now stoop to splitting absolutes. There are three types of evil in relation to fiction:

Evil *depicted* in fiction.

Evil *advocated* by fiction.

Evil *enacted* by fiction.

For clarity, let's turn to the principle of freedom of speech for an analogy. Freedom of speech obviously includes the right to speak *about* evil. Our own General Authorities devote a considerable amount of time to speaking about evil, from the evil of Communism to the evil of child abuse, from the evil of nonattendance at sacrament meeting to the evil of forgetting to pray.

And, under our inspired Constitution, I doubt that anyone would argue that we are not guaranteed the right to *advocate* evil, if we want. Any speaker may advocate any evil act. In America, a speaker may advocate revolution, crime, cowardice, dishonesty. In my own neighborhood in Orem a man has been going around urging people not to pay their taxes, a crime; no one stops him, because it's his right. In any society, what seems evil to one person may seem right and just to another—and in a free society, the government is forbidden to silence one and promote the other. Instead, each individual is expected to listen to all and make up his own mind.

But there is a third class—speech which in itself *enacts* evil. The traditional example is the person who shouts "Fire!" in a crowded theatre. He can call it a joke; he can claim that his freedom of speech allows him to lie; but in fact his lie, his joke, may cost people life or limb in the panic that ensues. Likewise, freedom of speech does not include the right to publish troop movement information in time of war, because it can cost life. There are times when some rights conflict, and a free society, to preserve itself, must place limits on its own freedom.

How does this apply to fiction?

All fiction depicts evil, but the mere depiction of evil is not wrong. And, because all fiction unavoidably expresses the moral convictions of the writer and because every writer will have different moral convictions, some fiction is bound to advocate things that at least some readers think is evil. But even that advocacy is protected.

It is only when the fiction actually enacts evil in itself that it becomes dangerous, and the government of a free society can begin to consider limiting it.

Pornography is the obvious case of fiction enacting evil. Pornography is designed to give direct or indirect sexual gratification. The appeal of pornography is not literary; though the writer may be skilled, the effect of pornography is not aesthetic, but orgasmic; it teaches the reader or the viewer to seek more such instant pleasure.

Pornography is merely boring to large numbers of people—they are not susceptible to it, just as many people in a crowded theatre will not panic and run for an exit when someone yells "Fire!" But for those who are susceptible, it can have serious debilitating effects. First, it is progressive. The regular consumer of pornography finds that what used to satisfy him now is boring, and he seeks ever more bizarre, brutalizing pornography to achieve his ends. Second, it is destructive, drawing the regular consumer into a fantasy world where women love to be treated cruelly and where the only good is self-gratification. Third, while pornography has never been proven to cause other sex-related crimes, it has been shown to accompany them. The sort of person who is likely to rape or murder or torture is also likely to be a consumer of pornography, and however the fantasies and the vicious reality may interrelate, it is difficult to extricate them.

But pornography of this sort is easily identifiable. It is aimed at a definite audience that wants it. The X rating sells pornographic films; the covers of the books leave no question as to what they are selling inside; whatever else they are, the purveyors of pornography are businessmen, and they advertise what they are selling to reach the market they want to reach. It doesn't take literary training to identify this kind of evil enacted by fiction—or rather, masquerading as fiction—to bar it from a community.

The problem arises when the untrained reader finds a passage describing a sexual event or a violent one in a work of fiction that is *not* aimed at the pornography-consuming market. Unaccustomed to reading at all, this would-be censor can only understand that he sees a pipe—he sees a sex act—and cannot see what purpose that depiction of evil might serve in the rest of the book. Reading *The World According to Garp,* he is incapable of recognizing that the lengthy kidnap/rape/murder passage is really satire by overkill; reading *Daniel Martin,* he is incapable of understanding that this character who seems to wallow in his mixed-up sex life, writing panegyrics on extramarital love, is really the author's tool in writing a beautiful defense of marriage and commitment. Unable to receive what the author is really trying to give, such ignorant readers are only able to receive such works as pornography. They have no perspective. They are like thirteen-year-old boys, their bodies stirring with the first urges of sexual drives that they will later learn to control, who lust after the buxom ladies in the comic strips and stare with guilty curiosity at the underwear ads in the Sears catalogue. They simply don't understand what's going on, and so everything they see looks provocative to them. The context is forgotten. They are children who simply aren't grown-up enough to handle the responsibility of judging what is really going on.

Things become more complex and yet much simpler in the area of evil advocated by fiction. It is simpler because it falls clearly under the area of freedom of speech. A writer can show people committing evil acts and living perfectly full, happy lives if he wants to. A writer can show righteous people as miserable, self-serving bigots if he wants to. A writer can even lie. It's his privilege, as long as he doesn't slander anybody who can get a good lawyer and sue. Eventually, however, a writer must be true to himself. It is impossible for a writer to convincingly violate his own conscience in his fiction. If he really believes that if you abandon your family you will become a hollow, miserable, unlikable character, it will show up in his fiction whether he tries to make his character seem happy and fulfilled or not. Eventually, a writer is forced to be honest to himself; even if he lies, the reader sees the lie, consciously or unconsciously, and rejects the fiction as false. The illusion of truth is lost because the substance of truth is inescapable.

But where writers honestly disagree with each other, their most truthful work will contradict someone else's dearly held beliefs. And that contradiction does not work itself out. The reader hears the ring of truth in works by writers with widely variant viewpoints. It can be confusing. Sometimes it can be infuriating.

And this is an area where some Mormons—and many non-Mormons—seem eager to lay the heavy ax of censorship as well. *The Prince and the Pauper* does indeed say that a vicious system has victimized those who are called criminals, and that fixing the system will cure the problem of crime. Mark Twain believed that, or believed in a great deal of it; and there are those—I think of a good born-again couple in Texas who provide a textbook-guide for born-again school districts—who want to ban such evil books because they have a ring of truth as they teach such things.

There are books that have a ring of truth to them as they teach us that an individual should forsake his commitments if they get in the way of his personal satisfaction. There are books that have the ring of truth to them as they teach us that sometimes a person just has to forget the laws and put a stop to crime himself, even if it means committing crimes to do it.

This was taken to absurd lengths recently when a television station yanked a program that some thought advocated teenage sex—in fact, it was a rather badly done attempt to show how much teenage sex can mess up a kid's life—and instead ran the movie *Dirty Harry,* which is one of the most sickening films I've ever seen in its celebration of vigilantism and violence. To one sort of a person, the change was obviously viewed as an improvement. To me, it was a definite step down. But the fact is that in a free society, advocacy of any viewpoint is protected, even in fiction. The writer of *Dirty Harry* has a right to make an American Stalin look like a hero, and I have no right to stop him, however I might disagree. However, I *do* have a weapon at hand—I can write my own book, and with any luck provide readers with a more powerful experience that leads to a different conclusion.

It is no accident that totalitarian countries invariably censor their writers, including—indeed, especially—their writers of fiction. The power of fiction to advocate particular viewpoints is astounding. Those who prefer to govern slaves know that when writers are free, the government cannot control the hearts and minds of its people. And that is why in our free society we cannot even silence those who advocate slavery—because their right to advocate the overthrow of freedom is what freedom is all about. If we were to silence them, we join them; if, to preserve freedom, we destroy, we have *become* the enemy.

Now That We've Dissected Evil, On to Truth!

Here is where we come to a particularly Mormon problem, where the issue of advocacy in fiction becomes complex instead of simple. Mormons, you see, *have* the truth. We have no doubt about what is good and what is evil. So we're perfectly safe in banning fiction that advocates evil—*we* run no risk of accidentally throwing out something good. With our perfect knowledge of the truth, we can always tell the baby from the bathwater. Right? I don't know if we can always be sure of that.

I was reading recently a book entitled *Roots of Modern Mormonism.* The author, Mark Leone, an anthropologist, had studied several wards in eastern Arizona, turning on Mormon society a carefully unbiased eye that sought to understand us, not from what we say about ourselves, not from what others say about us, but from what we actually *do.* The perspective was enlightening.

One insight from this book startles me, however. Leone said that Mormonism has remarkably little firm doctrine; that the variance of belief within the Mormon church is very wide; and that while Mormons are convinced that they have the complete revealed truth from God, in fact they have very few beliefs that are universally agreed upon.

That seemed impossible to me. But the writer had been so perceptive on other matters that I couldn't help but try to think where he might have gone wrong. It's an important question. If a large area of doctrine is not firmly established, then we would be treading on dangerous ground if we tried to ban writers who disagree with what we believe.

While we do have a core of absolutely certain and universally shared beliefs, there are many doctrines that have varied or changed over time, and many other doctrinal areas where there has been no general agreement among members and leaders of the Church.

Some examples of doctrines that have changed:

A hundred years ago in general conference, Apostles were preaching that polygamy was essential to salvation.

In the early days of the Church, the old *Lectures on Faith* clearly taught that the Godhead consisted of two beings, the Father and the Son, and that the Holy Ghost was the mind of God and Jesus Christ; and it was only well after the time of Brigham Young that the doctrine of the Holy Ghost as a separate individual was clarified.

It wasn't until the presidency of Wilford Woodruff that the doctrine of sealing was really understood; before that time, people tended to get themselves sealed to a great leader of the Church instead of to their own parents or grandparents, so that they would be assured of a noble lineage in the hereafter. It wasn't until the 1890s that the Church policy changed to the one we follow today, of sealing children to parents back as far as we can go.

In short, there has been a great deal of doctrinal change and development over time. And why should that disturb Latter-day Saints? We sing it dozens of times a year—"The Lord is extending the Saints' understanding." Line upon line, precept upon precept, we change our doctrines as we become better able to cope with greater light.

Yet, every time there is a major change, some few poor souls fall away from the Church. They splintered away when Joseph Smith misspelled their names, when Joseph Smith's bank failed, and when Joseph Smith edited his revelations. They splintered away when the Church abandoned polygamy, and when blacks received the priesthood before the Millennium.

These Saints forget that each living prophet speaks the word of the Lord to the people of his time. Today's prophet takes precedence over yesterday's. And tomorrow's prophet will supersede today's.

But the Church is not only diverse over time. It is also diverse among the Saints at any one time. In this room there are probably good Latter-day Saints who believe that the theory of evolution is perfectly compatible with the gospel—and equally good Saints who believe that the theory of evolution is directly contrary to scripture.

But the differences of opinion are not just among ordinary Latter-day Saints. Diversity of opinion has often existed at the highest levels of Church government. David O. McKay, for instance, believed firmly in the principles of geological time; in a speech at BYU he urged students to study many things, including the millions of years it took to create the earth. Yet President Joseph Fielding Smith held just the opposite opinion. It is no accident that at BYU, the Church's university, you can take a class in the Eyring Science Center where a teacher will quote David O. McKay in favor of evolution, and then you can cross the street and take a class in the Joseph Smith Building where a teacher will quote other authorities to buttress the idea that the earth was created in six thousand years. This disparity is actually official. President Joseph F. Smith, early in this century, issued an official statement of the First Presidency which affirms only that whatever the method he used, God created the earth, and mankind. It is not required that we agree on the details.

The disparity can amount to outright disagreement. At the end of World War I, President Woodrow Wilson was a fervent advocate of the League of Nations, believing that the League would be a potent instrument to avoid the kind of suffering and carnage that had virtually destroyed a generation of European youth. Church President Heber J. Grant and most of the General Authorities agreed. They spoke in general conference, in stake conferences, in wards, everywhere they could, advocating that the United States join the League of Nations because without our full entry into the League it would not achieve the objective of world peace. Some Apostles went so far as to preach that Woodrow Wilson had been raised up by the Lord for the purpose of establishing the League. There was no doubt in anyone's mind that the official position of the Church was to favor the League.

But in Washington, D.C., one of the senators from the state of Utah was Reed Smoot, a one-time student at this school, by the way. Reed Smoot was one of a group of Republican senators who perceived the League of Nations as a surrender of American sovereignty, which we should shun or hedge about with so many restrictions that the effect would be the same—the death of the League as an effective international policeman. It also happened that Reed Smoot was an Apostle. He held an opinion directly contrary to the expressed will of the prophet of God and directly contrary to the general feelings of the Twelve Apostles. Only a few General Authorities agreed with him—among them such loyal stalwarts as David O. McKay, Joseph Fielding Smith, Charles W. Nibley, and future General Authority J. Reuben Clark, Jr.

I think it is instructive to all of us to see what these loyal Latter-day Saint leaders did when they disagreed with the prophet of the Lord. Apostles on both sides conceived of it as a moral issue, and quoted scripture both to support and to oppose the League. At the height of the controversy, Elder Joseph Fielding Smith wrote a letter to President Grant,[1] which reads, in part:

> It appears that I am not in full harmony with the majority of my brethren. This is a solemn matter with me for I do not want to be out of harmony. I have but one desire and that is to support my brethren in defense of the truth and live in such a manner that I may at all times be in possession of the Spirit of the Lord. I have prayed about this matter and have lain awake nights thinking about it, and the more I reflect the more the position which I have taken [in opposition to the League of Nations] appears to me to be correct. Under such conditions I know of no one to whom I can go, only to you, and I do so in the hope, and I believe the confidence, that I will not be misunderstood and that you will appreciate the position that I am in.

---

1. Portions of the letter are quoted in James B. Allen, "Personal Faith and Public Policy: Some Timely Observations on the League of Nations Controversy in Utah," *BYU Studies* 14 (Autumn 1973): 93, 94.

And when the Senate vote for ratification of the League treaty came, Apostle and senator Reed Smoot cast his vote directly contrary to the publicly expressed will of the prophet and the majority of the Twelve. And in part because of his vote, the League failed.

What happened to these brethren who disagreed with their prophet? Charles W. Nibley was called a few years later to be President Grant's Second Counselor. J. Reuben Clark, Jr., later joined the First Presidency of the Church. David O. McKay and Joseph Fielding Smith were later Presidents of the Church. And those who supported the prophet were also, of course, in full fellowship with their quorums.

The clear lesson of this episode is that the Mormon church is a tolerant, loving Church, where people of sometimes diverging beliefs are joined by the all-important beliefs that we have in common. I won't list them for you—you memorized many of them in Primary. It is not only possible for loyal Latter-day Saints to disagree, even on moral, scriptural, and doctrinal issues, it is *likely*. We are not members of a common church because we are all adherents to a narrow catechism that precludes the possibility of disagreement or misunderstanding. What bonds us together in the Church is the brotherhood of Christ and our common goal of securing eternal exaltation for ourselves and everyone else who will receive it. The Church is inclusive, not exclusive; flexible and changing, not rigid and intolerant.

The extension of this to the matter of advocacy in fiction is obvious. Even within the Church, it is rarely necessary, desirable, or even possible to say that a particular work of fiction is indisputably evil and must be forbidden reading to Latter-day Saints. We are trusted to decide such matters of belief for ourselves. (The only time the Church acts to officially discipline people who oppose official Church positions outside those few areas where doctrine is firm is when those individuals cease to advocate their viewpoint and begin to directly attack the Church itself. At that point, such a person has already chosen to remove himself from the fellowship of the Saints, and the Church merely ratifies that individual's decision.)

The Lord defined truth as things as they are, as they were, and as they will be. But as long as we remain human, we are consistently at least one step away from that truth. In the search for truth, we have no direct contact with things as they are, were, and will be. Past events are relayed to us through observers, who, no matter how honest they were, still color their observations with their prejudices. Our own prejudices cloud our vision of things as they are. The prophets relay to us a vision of the future, but it is impossible to collate those visions into a clear, accurate forecast of all that will take place.

We discover truth through many means. Observation tells us not what happened, but what was observed to have happened. Generalization tells us not what happens, but what has always happened in similar or identical cases so far. Prediction tells us not what will happen, but what the evidence leads some individuals to believe will happen. Prescription tells us not what *should* happen, but what individuals *desire* to have happen. Whether it will really be good or not will only be revealed in the actual event.

Indeed, the shakiest of all approaches to truth is prescription, because it invariably depends on the accuracy of our prediction. When a doctor prescribes penicillin, it is because penicillin has been proven many times in the past to relieve the particular symptoms you exhibit. It is because of the doctor's prediction that penicillin will cure your ailment that he prescribes it.

There is a great deal of evidence to support the idea that penicillin is worth prescribing. However, when you move away from physics, chemistry, or the other hard sciences, prediction gets pretty shaky. Into the realm of history and politics and psychology and sociology prediction ceases to be what *will* happen—it becomes what *might* happen. Despite the much-vaunted repetitiveness of history, history does not repeat in detail. Empires may rise and fall along the same patterns, but in its relentless progression the event still unwinds one day at a time, and no two days are ever identical. So predictions of human behavior—those grand speculations on what *might* happen—are not based on experience of what happens every time the experiment is repeated. Those predictions are based on conclusions drawn from a collection of independent events that may or may not have a relation to the event in question. In predicting human behavior, we find ourselves relying on statements that boil down to what might have happened, what we *think* happened, and—the most dangerous of all—what would have happened *if only*.

If only. If only there had not been sex education in school, my daughter would not be pregnant. If only there *had* been sex education in school, my daughter would not be pregnant.

If only the textbooks could be brought into line, our children would not think incorrect thoughts.

If only the novels that show sex and violence could be banned, our terrible crime problems would be solved.

If only John Gacy's father had not been cold and distant from him, Gacy would not have killed a score of innocent young men.

If only we could get people to stop mentioning ugliness, the world would be beautiful.

So much prescription depends on that insidious phrase "if only." And yet "if only" contains two vicious lies that make that phrase the eternal enemy of truth.

The first lie is the word *only:* Its root is the word *one,* implying a singleness that never occurs in real life. It implies that a single change would have a single effect, which is absurd on its face—for instance, the popular lie that *if only* Chamberlain had not tried to pacify Hitler and instead had taken firm action years earlier to stop the Hitler menace, the Second World War could have been avoided. Isn't that nice? Isn't it pleasant to think wistfully about how easily such tragedy could be avoided, and how easily we could avoid it in the future? Yet Chamberlain's pacification attempts were themselves an effect, not a cause. If he had even suggested going to war with Hitler before the invasion of Poland, his government would have collapsed and the English would have replaced him with a government that would try, as he did, to avoid war. And if England and France had invaded Germany long before Hitler's buildup was complete, wouldn't we today condemn that action as vicious warmongering? There is no single cause of any event, and no single result from any change.

The second lie is the word *if: If* implies that the predictor has a perfect knowledge of the cause-and-effect chain. But that perfect knowledge has not been vouchsafed to any man.

That is one of the meanings of the veil that blinds us to eternal things. We live in time, day to day, and the world is narrowed to what we can perceive with our own senses and learn from those who teach us. If we had the perfect knowledge that God has, it would be no test for us here; we are kept in ignorance because only in that ignorance are we able to reveal to God and to ourselves who we really are. We do *not* know what would have happened *if only* we had done something different; we only know the desires of our own heart, and what our goal was when we acted. That is what we will be judged by—what we desired and tried to do. The intent and the act, but not the long string of consequences that extends infinitely from that act. We are not so implacable as the Greeks. We Latter-day Saints do not believe that God would punish Oedipus for sins he never desired to commit. "If only" has no meaning to us.

So why does anyone believe that if you can just keep children from reading about sex, they will never perform their own disastrous experiments? Long before there was such a thing as a novel, Europe was heavily populated with people whose coats of arms bore the bar sinister—illegitimate births and illicit sex are as old as mankind, and we writers of fiction are not the cause of them.

Why does anyone believe that if you can just keep writers from depicting acts of violence, acts of violence will disappear from our society? There were mass murders among the illiterate nobility of medieval Europe as rapacious knights pillaged their own people when they couldn't find any enemies to pillage. Ivan the Terrible needed no novelist to tell him how to be a butcher. Rape was not invented in the penny dreadful.

The depiction of evil in fiction is not the perpetration of evil. The mention of unpleasant things is not equivalent to their advocacy. Because in the novel I am writing now I will recount the murder of the Prophet Joseph Smith does not mean that I am consenting to his death. Those who, in the name of truth, would ban all depiction of evil are in fact the enemies of truth. Their motives may be good, but neither their goals nor their methods have any likelihood of improving the world to even the slightest degree.

A Lover of Goodness and a Student of Evil

All this puts the LDS writer in the anomalous position of being a lover of goodness and a student of evil. Because my fiction has to have the ring of truth, I must learn to write evil convincingly. I have never murdered, but I must understand the motives that can bring a man to kill. I have never committed adultery, but I must understand the motives that bring a man to break a commitment sealed not only by vows but also by years of shared experience. The terrifying thing is that I can find all those human motivations to do evil simply by looking into myself. The only solace is that I can also look into myself to find all the desires that prompt people to do good.

The *Lord of the Rings* trilogy is a textbook example of the problem of dealing with evil. John Ronald Reuel Tolkien was, of all things, a decent man. And look what he does with evil. Sauron isn't evil, he's just mean. He does nasty things, and we're never given the slightest clue of what motivates him. If it's good he destroys it. If he can't destroy it, he perverts it. But why? Tolkien just calls him evil and leaves it at that. It's a cheap way of dealing with evil—paint it black, make it do nasty things, and everyone will hiss whenever it comes onstage.

But Tolkien's Sauron and his little surrogates, the impish and absolutely unindividuated Orcs, are not where Tolkien really deals with evil. Even Saruman, the wizard of white who succumbs to the temptation of pride and turns to the pursuit of selfish ends, even he is shallowly treated and arouses little pity and fear in the reader. Where does Tolkien deal with evil well, believably, importantly? Primarily in Frodo, the protagonist. The good guy we follow from his first possession of the ring to his terrifying finale at the Cracks of Doom. Frodo, whom we weep for when he sails west with the Elves and leaves Sam Gamgee behind. Isn't it Frodo who wrestles with the temptation to throw responsibility on someone else and try to escape? Isn't it Frodo who at the end is overwhelmed by the power of the ring? Isn't it Frodo who is faced with the temptation to kill Gollum, and yet resists? Frodo's companion, Samwise Gamgee, goes through similar struggles with his evil desires. And in Gollum we find good and evil mixed, in different proportions, but still all there. These are the only complete characters in *The*

Lord of the Rings, and it is no accident that in Tolkien's strongly Christian viewpoint, it is these three weak and flawed individuals who, put together, bring about the supreme good act of the story. It is no accident that these characters, with their inward struggle between righteous and evil desires, are the ones best remembered and most loved by readers.

Like Frodo and Gollum, we contain within ourselves the desires for both good and evil. We children of God are not neatly divided into Elves and Orcs, some desiring only good and some desiring only evil. Such creations are only cardboard, thin and flimsy. It's a good thing Tolkien only sent one Elf on the quest—we would never have been able to tell two of them apart. Not only does a writer reach into himself to discover both good and evil, but also a writer's most believable characters will have those conflicting desires. It is not because the characters do evil that we find them interesting. We identify with them because we recognize both their good and evil desires in ourselves, and through their acts we learn the consequences of our own as yet unmade decisions.

Yet in my depiction of evil in stories and novels, I have never had any problem keeping that confusing mixture of good and evil in perspective. When my character sins, I don't have to tell the reader that his act was sinful. To me it seems inevitable that the adulterer pays the cost of his treachery, that the murderer loses his humanity when he takes another person's life so lightly. Without my even thinking about it, my innate sense of what is true shapes the plots of my stories and subtly preaches the moral values instilled in me by a lifetime as a Latter-day Saint.

Right now I am immersed in the fictional experience of a Latter-day Saint woman I've named Dinah Kirkham, who is reared in the terrible poverty of industrial-revolution Manchester and is brought by her new faith in Mormonism to America even though it means abandoning her children and her husband. In Nauvoo she becomes a plural wife of Joseph Smith; after his death, she marries Brigham Young and then lives to see her best-loved niece reject the gospel. In all the thousand pages of the novel, I never once even address, let alone attempt to answer, the question of whether Mormonism is really true or not. That is not what I'm writing about.

What I'm writing about is the way these characters behaved because *they* believed the gospel to be true. To abandon her family, to accept polygamy, Dinah Kirkham's faith has to be incredibly powerful; for the reader to believe her character, I have to make her motives utterly believable. When the reader closes my novel, he won't say, "The Mormon church must be true." But, if I do my job well, he will say, "Those Mormons were great people." More important, however, than the image of the Church that my novel will project is the fact that the novel inevitably projects my personal moral beliefs. Dinah Kirkham is a happy, admirable, secure person at the end of the book. She never loses her faith, despite her trials. Mormonism and the sacrifices the gospel called from her make her great. And in that sense, I can't help but preach the gospel. I believe that's the way the gospel works on the choicest spirits. I can't honestly write the book any other way.

Yet in this novel, as in every other story and novel I've written, I find that some of my most powerful passages are devoted to the depiction of evil. There is murder, there is rape; people are profane, people are cruel, people suffer, people inflict suffering. There will undoubtedly be some who read my work and misunderstand, like those few *Ensign* readers who did not comprehend the purpose of that pipe. Because they don't understand how fiction works, they'll see evil depicted and think it is advocated; they'll search for some overt statement of my testimony and never find it.

And this is something that a Mormon writer inevitably faces. When my play *Stone Tables*, with music by Robert Stoddard, first opened at BYU seven years ago, there were some who came and saw only that Moses and Aaron were portrayed wearing jeans, who heard only that the music was raucous and noisy. There were some who concluded that the play was obviously inspired by the devil, that it was evil and did not deserve a production at BYU. Yet seated in the same audience with them were people who did understand what Robert and I—and the cast and the directors, all faithful Saints—were trying to do. They received the play as it was given.

All this took place while I was on my mission. When I got home, a friend of mine took me aside and told me that when *Stone Tables* opened, she was only in Provo visiting; she had dropped out of BYU, and even though she had been baptized only a year or so before, her testimony had faded and she was convinced that the gospel was an empty promise that didn't deliver. Then she attended a rehearsal of *Stone Tables* and found ideas and feelings through the play that she had not thought of or felt before. She did not go home to California on schedule. She stayed and watched the play again and again. She remembered all the feelings that had led to her conversion in the first place. And she told me that the play had changed her life.

Of course, the play hadn't changed her; the Spirit of God changed her. But isn't it funny that night after night, when some people came to the show and found only the spirit of evil, right there in the same audience was a woman who found the Spirit of God?

The writing of fiction is a solitary act. The art of fiction really exists as immediately as theatre or film or a symphony—though the printed page can last for years, the story only lives when someone is reading it. The creative act of fiction depends as much on the reader as on the writer. It is not the presence or the absence of evil in the events recounted in the story that decides whether a work of fiction is good or not. What decides the moral value of fiction is the character of the person writing it and his skill in writing, and the character of the person reading it and his skill in reading. An evil writer will write an evil book; an untalented writer will accomplish little with his book, whether he is a good person or not; an evil reader will detect nothing but evil in his reading; and an unpracticed and unskilled reader will never discover what is really in the book, no matter how good his personal moral fiber might be.

And even that is too simple. However good I try to be, undoubtedly there are flaws in my character that I have not yet discovered or rooted out. Those will show up in my writing. And in even the most corrupt of writers, there are still remnants of righteous desires that will leave their clean traces in their work. Even if we could always be certain which writers are good and which are evil—and we can't; even if we could always be certain which of our personal beliefs are actually eternally true and which are in error—and we can't; even if with consummate skill as readers we could always be sure we had found every shred of good and evil in a particular work of fiction—

and we can't; even so, we would be foolish to set ourselves as judges over what people can and cannot write, and what they can and cannot read. For we never know which book, which offends us, might not contain that shred of truth that leads another person that much closer to happiness.

It is not inappropriate to think of books as children. Some children are obviously good; but there are others who bring their parents to the brink of despair. It seems they'll never amount to anything; they rebel constantly, deliberately choose evil at every opportunity. But if you had it in your power, would you even want to try to choose which children to allow to grow to adulthood, and which lives to snuff out before they do any more damage? Unthinkable. You never know what a child might become.

Only when the fiction ceases trying to be fiction at all, and instead has as its objective the gratification of the reader's basest desires; only when the fiction directly enacts evil instead of merely depicting it or even advocating it—only then does a free society have a right to protect itself at the expense of the freedom of the writer and reader to communicate as they wish.

But does that leave you defenseless against the advocates of evil? Of course not. There has never been a book written that has one-hundredth of the power in shaping human lives that parents exercise every day. You can combat the errors your children learn from fiction exactly as you combat the errors your children learn from their friends—by teaching them otherwise, by setting an example, by strengthening their conviction of and commitment to the truth; by loving them. In spite of that, some children inevitably choose evil because that is the desire of their hearts—but those who desire evil don't need fiction writers to teach them what evil is and how to get it.

And in the meantime, those of us who find much of our lives through the work of writers of fiction will continue to share the creative act of fiction. To some people we seem to be peculiar creatures, surrounded by books, spending hours of our lives in Tolkien's Middle-earth, in Hardy's Wessex, in Renault's Greece, in Tolstoy's Russia, in Singer's Poland, and in Walter's Wales. They cannot understand our eternal love affair with Captain Ahab, Samwise Gamgee, Hari Seldon, Horatio Hornblower, Lew Archer, Yossarian, Demian, Gabriel Oak, Bathsheba Everdene, the emperors Claudius and Julian, Von Humboldt Fleisher, and Rush-That-Speaks. To the overwhelming majority of Americans—and the overwhelming majority, alas, of Latter-day Saints—everything that I've talked about today, which I've treated with such importance, would seem quite trivial. Because, by their own choice, books are forever closed to them; they simply do not understand the major part that reading plays in a reader's life. And the non-comprehension goes both ways. I look at the people whose only brush with fiction is the emptiest of television shows and the most vacuous of movies, and perhaps a memory of Nancy Drew and the Hardy Boys in their childhood, and I do not understand how they survive.

Presented here in paraphrase are questions that were raised during the question-and-answer session following the lecture. The accompanying answers help to clarify the viewpoints expressed in the foregoing speech.

1. *In your lecture, you appeared to use the terms* evil *and* suffering *interchangeably. Don't you distinguish between them? Isn't it possible to show human beings suffering without showing evil?*

I was aware of my deliberate broadening of the term *evil;* what surprises me is that anyone was listening closely enough to realize it!

Yes, of course suffering is different from evil, though I believe that evil inevitably brings suffering. Much suffering comes from seemingly random events that are not caused by human beings, or that are only inadvertently caused. For instance, floods and fires, earthquakes and major depressions do not impinge on our lives at the deliberate instigation of other human beings. And fiction could indeed be written (and has been written) completely about a character's response to such natural disasters.

But that subject matter soon gets pretty thin, and to write only of natural disasters is, I think, to perpetuate one of the lies the world would like us to believe. After all, one of the most insidious beliefs in anti-Christ philosophy is the claim that man is victim, not actor; that all of man's suffering comes from forces which no man can control, and that therefore no man is blameworthy. If that were so, why would a just God presume to put men before his judgment bar? One of the most important doctrines unique to Mormonism is Joseph Smith's teaching that man was uncreated—that our fundamental desires *are* who we are, and neither God nor any natural force created those desires. We have always been ourselves, and therefore we are the only ones responsible for our own acts. God is not toying with his creations—he is trying to elevate and bring joy to his fellow intelligences. That view of God and man tells us that while natural disasters may cause us stress, we are individually responsible for our responses to that stress, and will be judged for them. And once again, a Latter-day Saint fiction writer is forced to present evil, unless he chooses to write only about characters who are already on the verge of being translated. Furthermore, a Latter-day Saint fiction writer is bound to present the truth that most human suffering is the result, not of natural events, but of human sin or human weakness. Otherwise, we again find ourselves blaming God for all that's wrong with our lives.

For this reason, I don't think the difference between suffering in general and suffering caused by evil is significant to a writer of fiction. All suffering eventually raises the question of evil. And since Latter-day Saint writers start from the position that man is responsible for his own unhappiness, and that man's unhappiness is inseparable from either his own evil or his response to the evil of other men, evil is especially forced on the writer who believes in the gospel.

2. *Aren't there ways for a writer to sidestep the depiction of evil, and merely leave it up to the reader's imagination, instead of depicting it?*

That depends upon the conventions of the audience. The writer must communicate. Eighty years ago, the audience knew perfectly well what the writer was leaving out when he said, "And upon what happens next we must draw the curtain." But today, the audience would reject such direct elision; and because they have become accustomed to graphic depictions of practically everything, they have a tendency to be unaware of subtlety—if it isn't shown, it didn't happen, so far as the reader is concerned.

This does not mean that a writer has to pander to the ignorance of his audience. It does mean, however, that a writer may have to depict more in order to communicate with most of his audience than some of his audience might think is necessary. In such matters a writer must be governed by his own sense of proportion and decorum. I have never written a scene in which I believed either sex or violence was provocative, though I have written scenes in which sex and violence take place. I have never included sex or violence at all unless they were strictly necessary in order to understand the character's subsequent actions. For instance, in *Saints* Dinah Kirkham is nearly raped in what I hope is a rather terrifying scene; in the first draft, I did not include that scene, but merely referred to it. However, readers of that draft made it very clear that because they had not actually experienced some of the terror of that scene, they were unable to understand Dinah's later actions in response to it. So I added the scene, still being very careful to make the scene frightening rather than arousing.

Of course, some readers will respond in the wrong way—it can't be helped. But I know my own intent, and I know that it works just the way I want it to with several intelligent readers. Beyond that, I can't be responsible for the individual responses of the readers, since I have no control over the frame of mind in which they approach the work. Certainly I don't advocate that writers of fiction depict evil willy-nilly; but then, a sense of proportion is required to write fiction at all, and the writer's handling of evil will be only one demonstration of that particular faculty.

3. *Isn't it possible for the constant reading of sex and violence in books that are* not *intended to be pornography to still have a deadening and brutalizing effect on readers?*

It certainly is. A steady diet of occult horror novels, for instance, is not exactly going to be conducive to the reader's being close to the Spirit of God. But that is not the decision of the writer—it is a decision of the reader. No one will be brutalized or deadened spiritually by reading any novel or story of mine; but there are some who might be offended; and there are some stories I've written which, if the reader read them over and over for months, would certainly have a harmful effect.

But the reader, not the writer, is responsible for the diet of fiction the reader chooses, just as the grocer is not responsible if one of his customers eats nothing but Twinkies and dies of obesity. The world of fiction provides opportunities for a well-balanced intellectual and emotional and aesthetic diet; it is up to the readers to choose wisely. Only if you believe the government should determine your daily menu can you consistently believe the government should determine what people can read—outside the realm, of course, of poisons both literary and culinary.

On Art, Morals, and Morality

A review of John Gardner's *On Moral Fiction*

In my undergraduate days as a theatre student at BYU, my friends and I had long conversations of the variety commonly known as "deep and meaningful" about art—no, pardon me, Art. (In such conversations, it is never said without the capital letter.) We pondered what Mormon Art was and whether it was possible; what was the difference between good art and bad; what was the obligation of the artist to his audience; and what was the obligation of the critic to art, the audience, and the artist. We reached no good conclusions, and the indecision I arrived at then remained until my reading of John Gardner's *On Moral Fiction* (New York: Basic Books, 1978).

Not that Gardner has all the answers. But he has enough of them that I found myself constantly wanting to read the book to somebody; I ignored my own ban on defacing books and underlined and tagged and starred copiously; I found myself elevated, inspired, and encouraged by the book.

Why? Heavens—I write science fiction, of all things. But writing is writing, and as Gardner points out, you cannot avoid teaching in art—the lessons *will* be learned by the audience, whether you mean to teach them or not, and it is the responsibility of artist and critic to know what lessons they are and make sure the art is good art!

Not that true art is didactic. "Didacticism and true art are immiscible; and in any case, nothing guarantees that didacticism will be moral. Think of *Mein Kampf*," Gardner says. "True art is *by its nature* moral." (P. 19, italics in original.)

But how do we define morality? Here is the crux of it, for Mormons, I believe. Gardner was not writing to Mormons—he was writing to literary critics, writers, students, and scholars, and in that world morality itself has become discredited as a notion. Instead, in a mistaken application of relativity, the literary world generally regards good and evil as irrelevant to art:

"The language of critics, and of artists of the kind who pay attention to critics," says Gardner, "has become exceedingly odd: not talk about feelings or intellectual affirmations—not talk about moving and surprising twists of plot or wonderful characters and ideas—but sentences full of large words like *hermaneutic*, *heuristic*, *structuralism*, *formalism*, or *opaque language*, and full of fine distinctions—for instance, those between *modernist* and *post-modernist*—that would make even an intelligent cow suspicious. Though more difficult than ever before to read, criticism has become trivial." (P. 4.)

With that audience in mind—essentially an atheistic audience, or at least one embarrassed to talk much about God where anybody whose opinion matters might hear—Gardner defines moral art as art that "seeks to improve life, not debase it. It seeks to hold off, at least for a while, the twilight of the gods and us." (P. 5.) He explains that "art builds; it never stands pat; it destroys only evil. . . . [It] is good . . . only when it has a clear positive moral effect, presenting valid models for imitation, eternal verities worth keeping in mind, and a benevolent vision of the possible which can inspire and incite human beings toward virtue, toward life affirmation as opposed to destruction or indifference." (Pp. 15, 18.) Art presents evil, but does not applaud it; art presents good, and identifies it as a worthy exemplar.

Mormons, of course, far too often have another view of moral art. It is art that could be presented in sacrament meeting—art that depicts nothing evil. Or, even more deplorably, it is art that depicts nothing but good.

I have run into this rather often. In my play *Liberty Jail* I attempted to show some of the rather unpleasant motivations that drove otherwise good people away from the Church. (Contrary to some childish oversimplifications I have heard, not all dissension within the Church is necessarily dissent from the gospel—sin is not always at the foundation of doubt or speculation, though sadly it is often their culmination.) The play was soundly criticized for showing such men as Sidney Rigdon in an unfavorable light during a time when they still held high position in the Church, as if they only suddenly apostatized, and did not have the seeds of apostasy in them even while functioning in office.

The criticism always boiled down to the idea that I had shown ugly things on stage. I had shown hatred and jealousy and greed and bad manners. Didn't I realize that a true Latter-day Saint artist would not make his audience think of ugly or difficult things, such as pondering the obvious fact that at various times in Church history people in high office have not been obedient to the prophet or aware of the Spirit of the Lord? It is the duty of the Latter-day Saint artist, I was told, to bring more beauty into the world.

The problem with this is Plato's old error that showing a good man doing something bad is bad, for it corrupts the morals of those watching. Perhaps the best argument against this fallacy is to show the absurdity of following it. If art only showed good men doing good and bad men doing bad, it would have no correspondence with reality, because there is no such thing as a wholly bad man (unless the Lord is wrong, and some significant percentage of men really can't repent).

Good men do bad things. In fact, I have known very good people, some of the finest people I personally know, who have, inadvertently or through momentary weakness, deeply hurt others or made terrible mistakes with far-reaching consequences. That is reality. For if Latter-day Saints look into themselves and see, as most will see, that they are basically good people trying to do right, and if upon realizing that they conclude that they are thus incapable of doing wrong because no storyteller has ever admitted to them that well-meaning people err, then the artist has reneged his responsibility and his audience is less moral, not more. They will be convinced that whatever they do is the sort of thing that good people do. They will no longer seek to repent of their own sins, but rather endeavor to make all other people identical to themselves.

On the other hand, if the storyteller has shown good people doing evil, then he has a chance to kindle within his audience the spirit of remorse. Sometimes the artist may show repentance; sometimes he may show the sinner destroyed by his sin; sometimes he may even show that the sinner seems to prosper while good people suffer. All of these, however, will certainly affirm in the good-hearted members of the audience a longing for repentance.

In short, it is the duty of the moral artist to affirm, to build, to construct—but one of his tools, one of his building blocks is ugliness. Beauty and ugliness are not opposites. As Gardner says, "The primary intuition of the poet-priest is one of a particular sort of order, an order which is partly sensuous, made up of objects loved or hated, partly transcendent and abstract, a vague but powerful sense of the general classes of things which *ought* to be loved or hated; in other words, affirmed or blown to bits. What he loves the artist calls beautiful; what he hates he has no word for (not 'ugly,' or 'grotesque,' or 'trivial,' or 'wicked'), he merely wants it *out*." (P. 156, italics in original.)

What matters is whether the story contributes to good order.

If a work of art depicts evil and shows it to be painful, unrewarding, negative, destructive, bad, then that work of art is exactly as moral as one which shows good to be beautiful, uplifting, desirable. Art is not moral when it never shows ugliness; art is moral when it shows ugliness *honestly*.

And yet so much of Mormon art shows good to be bad! That is, it often shows goodness to be puerile, or impossible, or—heaven forbid—boring. A gooey G-rated film that reduces goodness to niceness does as much harm as an R-rated film that makes evil seem rewarding, since both will move an audience to shun the good and espouse the evil.

Mormons have a tremendous potential for creating moral

art, as soon as we overcome our preoccupation with morality as a synonym for virtue. We waste too much time attacking pornography when we should be attacking soulless self-gratification in every form; trying to ban the R-rated film when we should be trying to protect our children from destructive worldviews whether someone has rated them with a letter or not. Anyone who has seen a predominantly Mormon high school classroom with its appalling lack of respect for the teacher and the subject matter can see that we may be keeping our children from dirt, but we are not providing anything to fill the vacuum. And as a matter of fact, good art does drive out bad as long as a society values goodness; only when we reduce art to the level of a political poster (you can't say *that*—it doesn't follow the party line!) does the public turn to whatever trash will, even momentarily, entertain.

That does not mean that I approve of pornography (though I, like every other person I know, have a private definition of what it is); instead my feelings rang in sympathy with Gardner's declaration: "I do object strongly to the cult of sex and violence, and more strongly yet to the cult of cynicism and despair, not that I recommend censorship. I am convinced that, once the alarm has been sounded, good art easily beats out bad, and that the present scarcity of first-rate art does not follow from a sickness of society but the other way around—unless, possibly, the two chase each other's tails. . . .

"Real art creates myths a society can live instead of die by, and clearly our society is in need of such myths." (P. 126.) Mormons can no more live by empty, meaningless art that pretends to be moral because it is devoid of any relation to reality than the rest of the world can live by art that scoffs at morality and presents a view of life as a meaningless, pointless, undirected accident.

Another tendency that weakens Mormon art is didacticism. I have too often heard the suggestion, always offered with good intentions, "Why don't you write a play (novel, story) that follows a character from the preexistence to this life and on into eternity to show the plan of salvation?" I usually answer politely, but my true answer is, "Because we do not live in the preexistence or in eternity, and furthermore I have better things to do with my time than try to rewrite abstract doctrines from the

Sunday School manual." It is, in my opinion, far more important for an artist to show the consequences of a man's acts than for him to inform the audience on theological principles. The storyteller's business is not the analysis but the experience of causal relationships. As Gardner says (and it seems I can quote him on every point), "Life is all conjunctions, one damn thing after another, cows *and* wars *and* chewing gum *and* mountains; art—the best, most important art—is all subordination: guilt *because of* sin *because of* pain" (p. 6, italics in original).

Gardner also decries the changing fashions of art—and too often Mormon writers are tempted to join these bright-painted bandwagons. Writing is made obscure because opaque writing is fashionable; plot is eschewed because no one would dare use suspense now (a tool of the pulps!); the trimmings, the style, the manner of the art become so important that the matter of the art is utterly lost. Yet the matter of the art is all-important. If it makes no difference to you whether you write about the day of a cow in Nebraska or the suffering of a man who has been excommunicated because of something he truly meant not to do, then you have no business in art: and if you value your style above the specific morality of your artwork, chances are your art will reflect that egoism and be, therefore, immoral.

A graduate writing student once said to me, "It doesn't matter what your story is *about* until you get a good style." I sincerely hope he finds his life's work in plumbing or computer programming, where he will find out right away that style is nothing and the job is only done when the product of his labor performs its function well.

Too often artists proclaim that they write only for themselves. "The writer may not care about any reader other than himself, but his work has no public existence except insofar as the feeling is not mutual. To say that one writes at least partly for others is not to say that one writes for everyone; one writes for people like oneself." (P. 20.) I like to think that every artist has an ideal audience, composed of people whose hearts resonate with the artist's work—provided they can find it, and provided that the artist himself has not interfered with the audience's ability to receive it.

Besides, my own observation is that the artists who proclaim most loudly that they care only about pleasing themselves are the ones most apt to follow fads and fashions in a desperate effort to please others. And even if the artist *is* being true to himself (whatever that means), sincerity is no guarantee of anything: "We have fallen into a commitment to sincerity rather than honesty (the one based on the moment's emotion, the other based on careful thought)—so that we admire more a poem which boldly faces and celebrates thoughts of suicide than we do a poem which makes up some convincing, life-supporting fiction" (p. 43). Besides, "the artist—even the essentially great artist—who indulges himself, treating his art as a plaything, a mere vehicle for his ego and abstract ideas, is like a man who uses his spectacles to swat flies" (p. 91).

The thrust of Gardner's book, however, is at the critic, whose responsibility it is to write criticism that "praises true art for what it does—praises as plainly and comprehensively as possible—and denounces false art for its failure to do art's proper work" (p. 16). The critic has tremendous power, since it is he who proclaims, Lo, here! and Lo, there! to the audience. If he doesn't point to good artists, they disappear: "Good writers, good painters, or good composers of whom no one ever hears do not, in effect, exist; so that whether or not those good artists are out there, we are living, for all practical purposes, in an age of mediocre art" (p. 56), primarily because of mediocre criticism.

"Most art these days is either trivial or false. There has always been bad art, but only when a culture's general world view and aesthetic theory have gone awry is bad art what most artists strive for, mistaking bad for good" (p. 16). And Gardner condemns us because we, as an audience, seek novelty, oddity, perversion instead of affirmation of good, enlightenment, morality. A depressing majority of Mormons who perceive themselves as intellectuals partake of this American disease, thinking all the while that it is a virtue. Mainstream Mormons, on the other hand, have an opposite but equally debilitating problem to beware of: a tendency to seek affirmation at the price of ignorance; cleanliness at the price of growth; comfortability at the price of having anything intelligent or honest to say. Both tendencies are immoral, because both lead artist and audience alike to be complacent in sin and comfortable with evil. There are many roads to hell, and Mormons have found some private ones that we have tramped down far too well.

PART THREE

The Artist in Mormon Society

Americans consume art at an astonishing rate, though most don't realize that that's what they're doing when they watch television, go to movies, or read magazines and books. American Mormons are scarcely different, except we have less free time. And I dare say that it might surprise you how many Saints *are* quite serious about the art they read and watch, look at and listen to. Almost from the time my books first started appearing, I have had calls and letters from people (almost always women) who are part of book-reading groups. Each month they all read a book and then meet to discuss it. And when I have been interviewed by such groups—by telephone, by letter, or, rarely, in person—I have found the participants to be keenly aware of some of the most significant issues in art theory and criticism, and to be perceptive readers of simple and difficult books alike. Usually, the members of such groups remain blissfully and humbly ignorant of just how intelligent and incisive they are. Most of them would say, "I just know what I like." What they don't realize is that they usually have very clear ideas of why they like it, and having passed through the furnace of many a graduate course in literature, I am quite confident that their reasons for liking or disliking a particular book are invariably at least as valid as any ideas I ever heard from the academic-literary establishment.

Even so, there is much confusion about what part an artist of any kind ought to play in Mormon society. I find it both amusing and disconcerting how often I have received letters that heap praise upon this or that novel of mine, only to end with some observation like, "I understand you used to be Mormon; when did you leave the Church?" When non-Mormon critics assume that in order to be an artist and a Mormon, I must be going through some torturous inner conflict, I can chalk that up to their ignorance of Mormonism. But why do so many Mormons assume that in order to write convincingly and passionately about Mormonism, I must no longer be an active, believing member? Why are they so astonished when, at various times, I have told them truthfully that far from being inactive, I was elders quorum president, choir leader, on the high council, Gospel Doctrine teacher, Sunday School teacher of the sixteen- and seventeen-year-olds, a bishop's counselor, a member of a stake mission presidency, an activities committee chairman, or director of the stake play? Why shouldn't a Mormon artist take part in the life of the Church exactly as a schoolteacher or a plumber or an insurance salesman or a lawyer is expected to?

The problem is not only with those Latter-day Saints who are not artists and assume that artists cannot be good Mormons. Unfortunately, far too many Mormon artists share that same opinion. They seem to expect that, as artists, they should receive some special treatment or be held to a different standard—one that gives them more freedom and less responsibility than other Saints. They have bought into the idea that having a talent or practicing an art allows them to be more critical of others while others must be less critical of them. I have found that the most common expression on the face of LDS artists when discussing ordinary, "unartistic" Saints is a sneer. So the lack of charity goes both ways. And I, for one, think there is no need for it. Both sides need to see things in a different light.

Oddly enough, in saying so all I usually achieve is to make both sides angry. I suspect that with these following speeches and essays, I'm about to do it all over again. But I hope not. I hope you will read with an open mind, for the subject does matter, to artists and non-artists alike.

Art as an Act of Charity

A speech given to the BYU College of Fine Arts, October 1990

It's good to be home again. I do a lot of speaking, but it's usually to non-LDS audiences, usually to people whose main interest is art alone, and to them I can't talk freely about half of what's important to me. Yet when I speak to Latter-day Saints, while I can talk about gospel doctrine, I usually can't talk about the artistic things that I care about. So today is a singular opportunity for me to be able to talk to people who are living in both streams of life that matter to me.

It's also good to be home in the Harris Fine Arts Center. I remember very well hanging out here as a theatre student in the late sixties. We were the obnoxious group sitting around the statue of Massasoit or down at the entrance to the Nelke Experimental Theatre, singing folk songs together and playing the guitar far more loudly than the faculty enjoyed. We were very aware in those days that outside BYU, students were rebelling against authority, dreaming of changing the world. We at BYU of course did not rebel; those who did, did not remain at BYU. But we did dream of being revolutionaries of another kind.

I remember very well that Dr. Charles Whitman, who taught playwriting then and still teaches here now, inspired many of us theatre students with a vision of Mormon theatre, of art created for Latter-day Saint audiences. But he wasn't the only one talking about it at the time. I roomed with four painters for a while, I had good friends in music and dance, and we were *all* talking about Mormon art. It was in the air then. We breathed it deep; we dreamed it. And some of us went on and lived it.

Sometimes we spoke of an even more daring dream: that what we did as Mormon artists could also be taken outside the Mormon community and change the world. Some of us lived *that* dream too. Maybe the world has changed only a little, but we *are* changing it.

When I talk to other writers about art changing the world, I will confess that a good many of them look at me rather strangely. "We just write stories," they say. "All we want is to get into the *New Yorker*. All we want is to create a little truth and beauty. We're not trying to change the world."

Everyone knows that artists don't change the world, they just get reviewed, right? Presidents, generals, lawyers, corporate CEOs—*they* change the world; artists just decorate it, right?

Wrong. We who learn to create artworks and share them with the audience, we *invent* the world. We put visions and music and stories into people's memories. Even when the audience for our works is small, they have received a priceless gift, for there is a place in their memories where, because of our work, all the people in that audience are the same.

Sharing the shaped reality of art is the closest we come in this world to truly knowing what is inside another person's heart and mind. For a moment, as an audience, as a community, we are one.

It's no coincidence that so much of Christ's labor in this life was devoted to creating works of art. His great atonement and sacrifice was and is an eternal act that transcends any mortal analogy. But of his other, more temporal works, which remain? The Church he founded eventually failed him. His doctrines were distorted, forgotten, and lost. His followers were slain.

The people he healed eventually died. But his stories, those deceptively simple parables, persisted. Where doctrines consisting of language can be and usually *are* reinterpreted into convenient new meanings, stories consisting of the causal relationships between events are very hard to reinterpret without the audience noticing and crying "Foul!"

We all know that the Savior's declaration "Upon this rock I will build my church" *can* mean different things to different people. But if I tell you that the "so-called Good Samaritan" was really a clever businessman who acted as he did so as to impress the innkeeper in order to get a purchasing contract with him later, and if I tell you that Christ's message was that you must do good PR in order to succeed in business, you *know* I'm lying. Clear, simple stories persist unchanged, where doctrines can be changed and *have* been changed constantly.

Among all else that he was and is, Christ was and is a creator, an artist, a shaper. And the stories that he told, though they were only heard by a few thousand people in a troublesome backwater on the edge of a desert (sound familiar?), have become part of the collective memory of billions of people. When Christ said, "I am the way," when he said, "Come, follow me," he was speaking as much to artists as to any other people.

It's really tempting for us as artists to start thinking that we're different from everybody else. Now, in some ways, we're *going* to be different; there's no way around it. We usually don't go off to a shop or an office to work. We're always home, and we look to other people as though we're unemployed. (Especially, I must tell you, that's how we look to bankers.) We have no bosses; no one assigned us our subjects without our consent. Our salaries are not weekly or monthly. (This is also not too impressive to bankers.) We get paid the way Death Valley gets rain. And then, completely unpredictably, our audience can suddenly balloon, and then our income resembles the rainfall in Amazonia—but we never know what made the difference.

We can't always produce on demand. Our work can surprise us. Nothing goes according to plan; nothing is predictable. We devote ourselves to strange disciplines. We see the world through different eyes. Without meaning to, we startle others with practically everything we say.

Yet didn't the Savior also step outside the normal track and live, as most of us do or will, from the generosity of people who love our words and our works? Our differences from ordinary people, our arts, should bring us closer to the Savior's way. Yet a disturbing number of LDS artists let their pursuit of art pull them away from the Lord and from the Church.

The Church is the community created by the Lord—more specifically, created by the Latter-day Saints under the authority of God. It is the tool we use to serve each other, to bring the gospel to the world, and to receive the Lord's guidance in our lives.

I remember when I worked in the Church Office Building as an assistant editor of the *Ensign* magazine, there were days—more of them than I am proud of—when I thought, "I do Church work every day of my life. Can't I have a day of rest on Sunday?" This rationalization became my excuse for not taking part in my ward in any meaningful way. I have since learned my mistake. The Church Office Building is *not* the Church. For every person there, as for every other Latter-day Saint, the Church is your ward or branch. And our identity within it is our calling which we faithfully fulfill. No one is exempt from this, and thank God for that. For no one is ever so wise or talented or important that he no longer needs to both give and gain through humble and faithful Church service.

Yet I have known too many LDS artists who feel that because they're artists, they need not walk on that strait and narrow road given to all the Saints. Instead they choose to walk on those broad roads leading to self-destruction. What they don't realize is that when they make those choices, they're not choosing art and rejecting religion; they're rejecting both their religion *and* their art.

Let me warn you today—because of course that's what you hoped for when you came, that you'd hear someone sermonize, and that's what I'm here for, whether you knew it or not—let me warn you today of seven temptations which many of you are already succumbing to, seven roads leading down to the river of filthy water seen by Nephi and Lehi. And then I'll have a few words to say about the inhabitants of at least one floor of the "great and spacious building."

The road, of course, is a metaphor. Your journey is through

time, not space. Your choice, then, is not made with the feet but with the heart. To choose a road is to give your allegiance, to take upon yourself an identity and system of values, a way of seeing your life in your work.

1. The first road is *allegiance to, or rebellion against, dead artists or dead art.* I like to joke that there are two reasons to get into art. The one reason is when you say, "Oh, I hope that someday I can do something that good." The other one is, "If *that* can get published or performed or shown, *I* can be an artist."

The first motive often leads the starstruck young artist to over-imitative work. The second can be just as deadly if it leads you to devote your career to reacting against work you disapprove of. (Frankly, though, I prefer the second motive, in part because it was my own.)

Of course, you *must* pay attention to artists of the past; it would be absurd to become so obsessed with originality that you failed to learn from both the achievements and the mistakes of your predecessors. Dead artists will teach you techniques. They will give you tools. They will inspire you with possibilities. They will warn you away from dead ends. But you must not allow their dead hands to define the boundaries of your work.

If you study art, you're only half-prepared to be an artist; you must also study life. And to know and understand life, you must take part in it. It's called *mimesis*: it is reality, and your relationship to it, that will teach you what your art should be.

When I was a theatre student, I resented all of the general education classes that took me away from my theatre work. They were a complete waste of time; I knew what I was going to do with my life, and my theatre work was what was preparing me for my future. Now, although I did learn much of value from my theatre studies, what I use the most, what is most important in my work, is the study and reading and experience that I've had outside my discipline. Technique is one thing. I have to also have something to write *about*. If you study only the works of artists, you may learn *how* to speak, but you'll have nothing to say.

2. The second road is *allegiance to your own career.* This is what the temptation sounds like: "If I can just get that NEA

grant, they'll *have* to take me seriously." Or, "You can't *do* that in this piece. The critic from the *Times* will be there, and he hates that." Or, "Don't tell your best friend about the party; he's so naive. He'd never make a good impression on all those gallery owners anyway."

The early Bolsheviks in Russia considered careerism to be one of the worst charges they could level against a fellow revolutionary. A careerist was a person who acted not to advance the Revolution but to advance himself to a more prominent or powerful role within the Revolution—and they were right. It was that careerist Stalin who transformed a brutal revolution into a monstrous one, and it was when the Soviet *nomenklatura* came to consist of nothing *but* careerists that Communism lost its last vestige of a claim to being a people's movement.

For a Latter-day Saint, careerism is always a mistake, and not just in the arts. What do you think David O. McKay was saying when he said, "No other success can compensate for failure in the home"? But for an LDS artist, it is even more important to avoid careerism, for careerism is what leads the artist to make cynical choices in order to go for the prize or the grant or the award or the good review. If your allegiance is to your career, you will sacrifice not only your religion but also your art in order to win these emblems of worldly success.

Now, I *have* received some of those emblems, because they are bestowed somewhat by chance. I can tell you by experience that, while they're nice, they are worthless compared to the non-career rewards. For instance, it's the letters I get, not often but sometimes, from teachers or parents talking about a kid or student who never used to read until he picked up one of my books, and now he's an avid reader. The highest praise I ever received came from a librarian at Farrer Junior High, here in Provo, who said, "Mr. Card, I have to tell you, *Ender's Game* is our most-lost book."

Those moments come to every sincere artist who is trying to tell the truth. But if you despise those rewards and seek the others, you're lost, because the other rewards are worthless. The world does not reward you for goodness, but good people do.

3. The third road is *allegiance to money*. Here's what the temptation sounds like: "You've got to have a chase scene."

Here's one I actually heard from several people not long ago: "We've got to change the protagonist to be sixteen years old instead of eleven; we've got to get the teen audience." I love that one. Or, "I can't sell *this* piece, but if you do more of those landscapes out of horizontal lines, I can sell millions of those."

Pursuing money is not the same thing as careerism. The careerist aspires to prestige, the honors of men. The greedy artist compromises to get a buck.

Now, I don't mean that artists shouldn't earn money at their art; the laborer is worthy of his hire. All people are expected to provide for their own needs and the needs of their families. Starving as an artist isn't a virtue, just a fact of life.

There are reasonable compromises and destructive ones. If you put off doing the project dearest to your heart in order to complete a less dear but still worthy project that will put bread on the table, that is not selling out; that is being a grown-up, especially if you have a family. When you fulfill the decent requirements set by the person who commissioned a work of art, that's not selling out; that's giving fair value. But when you produce art that you are or should be ashamed of because you think it will make you more bucks that way, then you are a prostitute.

And here's the ironic part. Not very far along that wide road it drops off into an abyss, because you soon forget how to tell the difference between good work and money-work. Soon enough the audience will recognize your cynicism and desert you. While those artists who *don't* compromise may spend years of sacrifice, yet still, eventually, if they really are good at their art, some decent money at least will usually come—or at least enough honor from good people that all the sacrifice will be justified.

Remember, though, that you are able to judge only your own decisions along this line. It's too easy to assume that anyone who makes money must have sold out. It's the cheap judgment. What looks like greed in someone else may not be greed at all. For instance, I used the word *abyss* a moment ago, hoping for the reaction that I heard—a little murmur here and there. I wrote a novel adaptation of Jim Cameron's movie *The Abyss*. Many people have assumed, because I wrote the novelization, that I must have sold out. What they don't realize is that not everything that comes from or is associated with the movies makes money. The usual payment for a movie novelization is pathetic. That's why novelizations are almost always done by new artists.

I made a good deal *less* money—and knew from the beginning that I would make less—doing that book than doing a book of my own. Furthermore, it took twice as long and was much harder to do. But I did it because Jim Cameron, the author and director of the film, and I both wanted to see if it could be done, if a good novel could be adapted from a film as so many good films have been adapted from good novels. We think we succeeded, though it took extraordinary effort on both our parts.

But it's worth knowing, I think, that what looks like selling out isn't always. Sometimes it's a sacrifice for the sake of some kind of weird artistic experiment. As to whether it succeeded or not, or was worth attempting—well, you're free to have your own opinion, as I have mine.

4. The fourth road is *allegiance to elitism.* Here is what the temptation sounds like: "Oh, I didn't expect *you* to understand my art." Or, "Did you get my reference to Jackson Pollock? Yes, down here in the right-hand corner." Or, "I could always work with traditional melody and instrumentation, but *that* stopped interesting me in high school."

In literature, it began with T. S. Eliot self-consciously writing poetry that was designed not to be understood except by the elite handful of people who had read all of the same books as Eliot and his friends. It was continued by James Joyce, who wrote great works whose primary pleasure came not from the experience of the story but from the decoding of the language. The untrained audience was deliberately excluded, and that was one of the primary pleasures of reading it—knowing that no one else on your block was fit to appreciate it.

The same thing happened around the same time in every other art, and prevailed in most of them. Non-representational visual arts and non-melodic and disharmonic music discarded the very reasons why most of the audience throughout the history of the human race had ever valued those arts.

Because the practitioners of the new elitism were able to come up with convincing critical stories, enough critics, dealers, buyers, and institutions that went along with the elitists were also able to make money. That didn't happen with the extremely expensive collaborative arts of film and theatre, and therefore they have not become dominated by the elitist viewpoint—though the elitist viewpoint does thrive.

In other arts, however, elitism's triumph is almost complete. Serious poets have taught the American public to detest poetry, so that now poetry is usually published in magazines read only by other poets who are trying to figure out how to get published. This is a tragedy, because the people have been cut off from many of the best artists, and many of the best artists have been cut off from the audience they really want to be speaking to.

But the people do still hunger for those arts, and if the serious artists won't give them to the people, the people will get those arts somewhere else. For instance, book covers, record jackets, calendars, prints of wildlife art are satisfying their hunger for visual arts. The public is very careful, very discriminating in their tastes. Without any official critical guidance, the public chooses the best—but they define "the best" by standards of their own.

The hunger for poetry and music is now satisfied through the American popular song, which, by the way, we sell a lot more of to the rest of the world than we ever do of our serious work. And there is more variety within that popular-song tradition today than in the world of so-called "serious" poetry and music. And there's a public with more emotional involvement and hype-proof critical judgment than within the worlds of "serious" poetry and music.

You may see a lot of hype, a lot of advertising, in popular music, but the public is virtually immune to it, ignoring many well-hyped artists while seeking out and discovering many who are hardly hyped at all. That almost never happens in the world of serious art. The hype *must* be there for the "serious" artist to thrive.

Now, I don't say that these serious arts are intrinsically bad. Every artist has a right to find an audience for whatever art he believes in and cares about. And every audience has a right to its art. The place where I argue with the elitists is their elitism, not what they do in their art. I dispute their claim that "serious" art is the only art worth paying attention to, or even worth doing in the first place. I rebel against their snobbery, for their attitude is poisoning us all.

The elitists have managed to persuade even the people who *hate* their art that their art is in some sense "better." Students learn that if a book or poem is "good" they'll hate it, and if they like a book or poem it must be trash—the teacher says so. And then people wonder why Americans don't read.

Worst of all, whole generations of artists are made to feel like failures or dropouts if they decide to create art for a wider audience than a handful of overtrained professionals. Many who might have stirred millions with their music or their art instead devote all their talents to pleasing an audience so jaded that the art will never have the power to win their love; the best it can win is their admiration. For where the untrained audience is always open to being transformed, the elitist audience is willing only to be impressed.

And the elitists know it. Their envy of popular art is palpable. Why else do they devote so much effort to sneering at the "mindless" mass audience and the "hacks" who try to please them? But I tell you that there is no higher percentage of talentless, cynical, careerist, greedy hacks among popular artists than among so-called serious artists.

And where do the elitists get off calling themselves "serious artists" in the first place? Do they think the rest of us are kidding? The true name of popular art is *democratic* art—art that speaks to the people, while the elitists speak to each other. They're free to do so, but they are not free to say that the elitist audience is the only one worth pleasing.

Quite the contrary. The elitist is the *least* important audience, because it is the one least open to genuinely new voices. In the world of democratic art, change and innovation are constant through a process of perpetual dialogue with a passionate audience. In the elitist world, techniques first used in 1920 are *still* called "modern" and "experimental." It's a closed shop. Conform or die.

Just remember, please, that Christ did not preach to the Pharisees; he preached to the common people. To a Latter-day Saint artist, enough said.

5. The fifth road is *allegiance to mysticism.* Some people think that the ability to create art is somehow magical, a gift of

the muses. Not only do they treat old works of art with awe, but many also treat their own words with the same mystical respect.

"I don't know why I did it that way, it just came to me." This attitude would be harmless enough if it didn't seduce so many artists into thinking that they themselves are some kind of *bodhisattva*, an incarnation of the gods of art. Too many artists think that, as artists, they are so precious and special that ordinary rules just don't apply to them. If an ordinary man abandons his family or verbally abuses his children, he's scum. But if an artist does it, he "needs his space." If an ordinary man takes drugs or drinks himself into oblivion, he's an addict or an alcoholic. If an artist does it, he's "tormented."

In defense of this view, people point to artists like Faulkner or Hemingway or Fitzgerald and say, "Look, he's a genius and see how he drank. See how he was eventually destroyed, or driven to suicide." What people often forget is that it is far more likely that Faulkner created his finest work *in spite* of his alcoholism; that it was the responsible, adult side of him that created his art, in constant battle with the self-destructive temptations of the flesh. It was not the creative part of Hemingway that pulled the trigger. Who can guess how much better their art might have been if they had mastered the flesh? The laws of God are natural laws, and artists are no more immune to the consequences of weakness, fear, or evil than to the law of gravity. The Lord and the law are no respecters of persons—artists are not and cannot be a special case.

Artists have no mystical connection with the divine, except the one that is available to every living soul, the one that was given to us through the atonement of Christ and the witness of the other Comforter.

6. The sixth wide road is *allegiance to style over substance*. I recently was talking with a young graduate in an MFA writing program at the University of North Carolina at Greensboro, who actually said to me (and I looked very closely to see if he was joking because I couldn't believe he was saying it, but in fact he meant it with his whole soul), "I wish more people understood that what matters most is getting a good style. Why work on what the story's about until you've learned how to write well?"

That's the attitude that has given us so much stylish, empty art in recent decades. It is all-pervasive in the artist community. Many people were recently appalled when an art critic testified that a photograph of a man urinating into another man's mouth should be received only as a "study of light and shadow." Both the audience and the artist are insulted by such a claim. Light and shadow might have been part of the photographer's technique, but *he*, at least, was not such a fool as to imagine that his subject matter was not important to his art. By making perversion fascinating and aesthetically pleasing, and by putting into the audience's memory an experience few of them would ever have conceived of without disgust, he *was* changing the world. The substance was what mattered to him. Remember that. Learn from Mapplethorpe if from no one else. Art only has power to change the world when it is *about something*.

Your technique will never be perfect. Never. But if your message is powerful and true, then your technique only has to be good enough, and your stylistic flaws will be forgiven. On the other hand, no matter how lovely your style, if your work has no substance, no subject matter that matters in the real world, you deserve to be forgotten, and I promise that you will be.

7. The seventh road is *perpetual adolescence*. This is what the temptation sounds like: "This will make those Relief Society ladies drop their teeth." It's what I call the "aha syndrome" among naive young LDS historians. When they first find something in their research they didn't read about in Sunday School, they crow, "Aha!" and they rush about telling everyone that they've discovered "the truth about Mormonism." And if you point out the flaws in their reasoning, then you obviously aren't ready yet to "face the truth."

It's the same adolescent desire to shock, the one that makes you do things that drive your parents crazy, for no other reason than to drive your parents crazy. We've all done those things. It's part of being an adolescent. It's part of separating yourself from the community that you grew up in, so you can find your own identity. But you're supposed to grow out of it.

You're supposed to spend your adolescence in a situation where the world is negotiable and your identity is in flux, until you discover who you're supposed to be. At that point you're supposed to become a grown-up.

A grown-up is a person who voluntarily commits himself to a community and makes a commitment that he will *never* break. That's the commitment you make when you marry and have children. Many *do* break it, but they shouldn't be proud of it. It's the commitment you make when you join the Church. Many of us do it young, of course, and so we have to make the commitment all over again when we're older. But the commitment must be there, or you are not adult.

That commitment means that when you find a problem, you don't stab the audience with it and gleefully rub salt in the wound while they howl. Instead you study it carefully and present what you've learned in a way that will hurt as little as possible—or, best yet, in a way that will affirm and strengthen the community.

The fact of the matter is that if you tell the truth, some of your audience will always be shocked anyway; you don't have to try to soup it up. In fact, you have to labor in the opposite direction: to soften the blow, not just to help the community, but also to help keep your audience open to *your voice*. You must lead gently, must offer milk before meat.

Christ's doctrine was hard, rigorous, shocking; but he taught with gentleness, meekness, and love, in the language of the people, according to their understanding.

Those are the seven wide roads that I've seen lead to the destruction of Latter-day Saint artists. And now we come to the great and spacious building beside the river, to one particular floor of that building, where you find the artistic/critical/academic establishment—the so-called arts community. There are exceptions among those who belong to that community, but in general, its members will labor to entice you down all seven of those roads leading to destruction of you and your art.

They encourage you to imitate dead artists, or at least to study them seriously, in part because they've already *tamed* those artists. They already have stories to account for everything they did. These much-studied artists are domesticated, and they can't argue against stupid critical theories about their work, because they're dead. And if the arts community can get you to believe their stories about the dead artists, and then to imitate them, then they've tamed you, too.

They encourage careerism because, of course, they're the

ones passing out the honors. If you live and die for their prizes, you will be utterly dependent on them; you are much more likely to conform to their idea of what is art.

They *talk* as if they despise money, and they accuse anyone who makes money of selling out. Yet money is what they love most and what most impresses them. I can only tell you my personal experience. (Actually, I *can* tell you other people's experiences, too, but I *will* only tell you my personal experience.)

Science fiction, of course, is *not* taken seriously in the world of letters and serious literature. But you would be amazed at how my reception in those circles has improved since I've had some books that hit best-seller lists, and since I've received some awards. I am no better writer, I don't think, than I was before, but it's amazing how much respect you receive, even from people who officially despise your art, if you've made some money at it. Don't believe their pretense. You'll wow them if you make the bucks.

Elitism is their lifeblood. They will try to persuade you that the world elitist art is intrinsically better than the best democratic art. They want to believe this because it's very comforting to them. You see, by this theory they don't actually have to be any good. They only have to belong to the club, and automatically their work will be taken seriously. All these naked emperors, vaguely aware that the others have no clothes on, but quite convinced that they themselves are gloriously attired.

They encourage artist worship, because it means that they can live as parasites in the gut of society without making the slightest effort to produce anything useful—or even to refrain from doing harm. Art is their blank check, because artists are "special."

They thrive on superficiality. It means that they don't even have to reach for wisdom; they only need to echo received opinion with flair.

They encourage perpetual adolescence and glorify it in their work; that's why we have these endless fictions about people "breaking free" of their "limiting" family life or their "limiting" job—in other words, fiction that glorifies people who abandon those who need them and count on them, those to whom they've made commitments. I wish I had a dime for every book like that that's going to be published this year. Why does the arts community hunger so much for this story? Because it allows them to excuse themselves for behavior that in non-artists would be despicable.

The arts community is eager to convince you to join them, especially if you have talent, because, unconsciously at least, they know they're empty as a society. If you join them, if you with your talent join them, it validates *them*. They'll try to convince you that it's *you* who's getting validated, but it's not—it's them.

And if you reject them, it stings them to the heart. Like hurt children, they seek to enforce conformity with ridicule and laughter and scorn—just like the people on every other floor of the great and spacious building. And if you let them make you ashamed, you will end up following one of those broad roads. Your gifts will end up being wasted, lost in a river of dirt.

And I must warn you, if you haven't already noticed it, that the arts community is not just "out there" in "the world"; it's also in here, inside the LDS community. Again, I do not speak of *all* LDS artists—by no means. But the people who consider themselves to be part of the LDS arts community draw their primary values from the world, not from the Church. They will ridicule you if you try to create art for the Saints. They will honor you only if your work is elitist, shocking, anti-democratic. They start from the assumption that if the common people love it, it must be lousy.

Often they are superficially right: the common people love it and it's lousy. But the people don't love it *because* it's lousy, and they don't hate the elitist stuff because it's good. They love the lousy stuff because at least it's speaking to them. They'd love better works if only the artists would offer them.

Let me give you a quick example.

Shirley Sealy. How many of you know her name? Ah, the hands rise, mostly women—that's one of those facts of life in the world of books. You may not know that along about the middle of the 1970s, Mormon fiction did not exist for the Mormon public at large. There were Mormon novels, but by and large they were aimed at a non-Mormon audience, and often they were attack fiction, designed to show you exactly why Mormon society is corrupt, evil, terrible, awful, and foolish. There were exceptions—I think of Don Marshall's *Rummage*

Sale as an excellent exception to that, and it was also a popular book. But Mormon fiction did not exist as a legitimate publishing category. Deseret Book and Bookcraft were sure that Mormon fiction wouldn't sell—so, of course, they published almost none of it.

Then Shirley Sealy came along with a book that, I must confess, I could not get more than twenty pages into. But that's a matter of personal taste. The book was clearly not written for me—I was not part of its natural audience. Many other Saints, however, *were*.

No one knew that in advance, however. None of the major publishers in the LDS market would touch it—they knew that fiction didn't sell, and I suspect none of the editors particularly enjoyed the book. It was a sure thing that none of the New York publishers would touch it.

But Sealy overcame that seemingly insuperable barrier, with the help of some good people who believed in her art, who believed that there was an audience eager for positive Mormon fiction. It was published by the Seventy's Mission Bookstore, and to everyone's surprise it sold like crazy. Whatever else you may think of it, Shirley Sealy's first novel created Mormon fiction as a viable commercial category. Her book made it possible for Latter-day Saints to go into a bookstore and find a wide variety of books by many authors—more all the time.

Yet when *Beyond This Moment* was first having its phenomenal success, many people reached an absurd conclusion—that because the first Mormon fiction to sell well was not very well written, you had to write badly in order to sell to the Mormon audience.

That wasn't the truth at all. The lesson they should have learned was that the audience was so hungry for fiction that they were willing to forgive flaws of technique in order to get fiction that spoke to them as believing, committed Latter-day Saints. Yet the same publishers who once were so sure that Mormon fiction wouldn't sell were then just as sure—with just as little evidence—that the only Mormon fiction that could sell was the same kind of so-called "women's book." There seems to be no master key to open all the doors in the house of art. You may open one door, but you'll still have to struggle to open the next.

I have put my money where my mouth is. I've made an expensive bet that there's an audience hungry for entertaining, affectionate, insider LDS fiction that nevertheless has very sharp teeth. I published a book called *Paradise Vue* by Kathryn H. Kidd, a book that I think achieves my goal of creating a sort of Jane Austen for the Mormon audience. This is a novel that would never have been published by the major LDS houses, because it shows too many of the warts and foibles of the LDS community, the way Jane Austen and Mark Twain and Charles Dickens did with *their* people. It also would never have been published by one of the houses that goes for fiction that either attacks Mormon culture or sneers at it, because this novel is so positive toward LDS people and values and doctrine.

The response that we've been getting to that book tells me that I was right, that once again there was a kind of fiction that the audience was hungry for but nobody was giving it to them. The response we're getting from readers is: "Finally, a Mormon novel I'm really glad I read." Now, obviously, there are people who are perfectly happy with the Mormon novels that are already out there—but then, I didn't mean to start a publishing company to produce anything for them; their needs were being met. The point I'm trying to make is that when the people are hungry, satisfying them does not mean you have to create bad art. It merely means you have to create good art that they know is directed to them—art that they can understand, believe in, and care about. And they do notice the difference. They are very, very discerning. Anyone who ever tells you that the mass audience only wants trash is speaking, not from an ivory tower, but from a window in another kind of structure.

How, then, do you avoid the pervasive influence of the great and spacious building, both inside and outside of the Church? How, as an artist, do you remain immune from that influence?

First, it takes toughness; you just have to be strong.

Second, you must remember, don't be ashamed of Christ. If, in your heart, you know you truly serve and follow him, then you will be comforted in spite of whatever ridicule and criticism comes your way.

Third, get a life. And I mean get a life in the ward among ordinary, common Latter-day Saints. Be friends, *true* friends, with non-artists. They will love you for much more important things than talent. They will be your friends even if you fail. And if you create your art with those non-artist friends in mind, they will teach you how to speak to the largest possible audience that can receive your uncompromising truth. Furthermore, they will teach you what real life is, so that your work won't always have to be about art or artists.

Let me offer you a slightly outrageous suggestion. To practice Mormon art, or to be a Mormon artist who keeps his or her soul, I suggest leaving Utah if possible. I've done art both in and out, and I'll tell you, it's easier to create good art outside. It's easier when you go to where LDS artists are rarer. I even went to a place where artists are rare, period. Greensboro, North Carolina, is not, I assure you, a mecca of fiction writing.

As a Latter-day Saint, it's good to live in a place where wards are more all-inclusive. In Utah, wards tend to be your neighborhood, with practically everybody in the same economic stratum. If you go somewhere else, you're likely to find a ward that will include rich and poor, white-collar and blue-collar people in every ward. Believe me, the Church is healthier that way.

Most important to you as an artist, you need to go to a place where wards are hungrier for any Saint who will fulfill a calling. When I lived in Orem, Utah, the ward leaders could never figure out what to do with me. The only calling I ever got, after waiting for months without one, was teaching the nine-year-old Primary class. I loved that calling, but I only got it because I begged for it—they offered it to my wife, who already had several callings!

The kids were great, and I still remember that as one of my best experiences in a Church calling. But the point is that until I begged for that calling, nobody could figure out what to do with me.

In Utah, you see, there are so many Mormons that most wards feel they can simply ignore the ones that are too strange. (It was 1980 and I was also a Democrat; that was a complicating factor.) But let me tell you, in Greensboro, North Carolina, and before that when we lived in South Bend, Indiana, they had callings for me. Why? Because where Mormons who will faithfully fulfill a calling are more rare, where wards include all kinds of people, you start judging people by different standards—better ones, I think; standards that are more in harmony with the gospel. Outside of the Mormon corridor, no faithful Latter-day Saint is regarded as expendable. They may still think I'm strange—and I am—but when I do my callings, they accept me as one of the fellow citizens of the Saints. I am part of the life of the Church as I never was able to be here.

Even if you stay here in Mormon country—and many of you will—you can still do some things that will help you live a real Mormon life:

Don't cultivate weirdness. Trust me, you're going to be weird anyway; you don't have to try. Instead, try very hard to appear normal. It communicates a good message. The message is: "I want to be one with you." And, of course, to the artsy types, it says the opposite, and that's also a good message to give.

You must absolutely forbid yourself to sneer, especially at things you don't understand. If you don't understand what people are reading those "silly sentimental Mormon romances" for, then don't you dare criticize them for it. You don't know what hungers are being met by that art. All you can truthfully say is that you're not part of the audience for that work.

Above all, when you look at the Mormon people, always feel yourself to be one of us—especially when we drive you crazy. Instead of saying, "Look at what those bozos are doing now," you must phrase it this way in your own heart, "Why do *we* keep doing these crazy things?"

This is not a matter of "mere" words; it is not a trivial difference. You must always conceive yourself to be part of this community, even when you disapprove of what the community does. Your sense of "us" must always include the Church, never exclude it.

And your sense of "I" must always include the Savior; that's what it means to take upon yourselves the name of Christ. He'll never sign your work, but he'll be part of it all the same. And then all your works can honestly be offered like prayers, in the name of Jesus Christ.

Sermons in Critical Form

A response (written in April 1982) to a review in the *Sunstone Review*

Susan Wakefield's recent review of *Charly* and *Sam* ("Sermons in Novel Form," *Sunstone Review* 2 [January/February 1982]: 24–25) is unfortunately typical of a view that far too many LDS litterateurs espouse. Having learned critical method in the Modernist tradition, they judge Mormon writing by the prevailing standard of the day, instead of judging the prevailing critical method by the standard of Mormonism. The result is that Wakefield has actually criticized Jack Weyland's novels because they take place, using Susan Howe's words, "within the context of Mormon cultural myths." The sin that Weyland and his ilk have committed is "using literature to validate our culture rather than explore it." I wonder where it is engraved in stone that a writer who is telling stories to his own people has to pretend not to believe what he believes in order to do it well. One might as easily demonstrate that the greatest writers—for instance, Homer, Sophocles, Shakespeare, Dickens, and Twain—have written to both validate *and* correct their community.

What matters is not whether they affirm or attack, but that they are members of the community writing *as* members *to* other members.

The problem with judging Mormon writing by outside standards begins with the Modernist demand for objectivity, distance, detachment. The premise here is that the value of fiction comes from its "meaning." Meaning, unfortunately, is not neatly detachable from a work, unless someone taught the writer to put it in that way. When a critic goes hunting for meanings, he is likely to find, not what is in the text, but what he puts into the text. Stories are experienced, not deciphered—*discourse* is deciphered. Translating stories into discourse makes them not-stories. Such a critical method does not examine fiction; it instead creates discursive paraphrases of it, translations in another form that cannot possibly duplicate the effect of the original story.

It is ironic that this critical method forces the solemn critical reader to extract sermons from stories. This is precisely what Wakefield has done with *Charly* and *Sam*. Her literary approach is based upon the notion that meaning must be found in stories and evaluated. She only calls the meanings she finds in these books "sermons" because she does not like them. If Weyland had instead clearly taught messages she approved of, she would probably have called them "significant and telling commentary on Mormon society" or "profound explorations of the Mormon myth." Your messages are shallow sermons. My messages are enlightening insights.

"The meaning of a story" is a nonsense phrase anyway, when used with the definite article. A story is not properly received as discourse on a theme; a story is received as an experience, as vicarious memory of causally ordered events. Reading a story is not analogous to reading philosophy—it is analogous to the way we experience other people.

In life, we think we "know" other people because we can see them. In fact, however, all we know of them is what we remember of them and the stories we tell ourselves about them. Each time we meet them, our image of our acquaintances changes, partly because each new experience affects the overall impression we have, partly because we ourselves have changed. However, our previous conceptions of people also, in large measure, create our impressions of them in the first place. That is, our unconscious decisions about what is important about their behavior and what is trivial, what is "really" them and what is just an aberration depend on the story we told ourselves before we even met. We apply names to people immediately: white or black, woman or man, Mormon or non-Mormon, Rotarian or non-Rotarian, educated or ignorant.

We go through the same process with stories—and with the characters in those stories. Wakefield obviously approached *Charly* and *Sam* as she began her review: The most interesting thing about them is that they sell very well. By Wakefield's personal inclinations, she probably would never have read them. "Weyland has apparently captured the formula for best-seller Mormon fiction." If the books sell well, they must do so, by definition, through finding a "formula." Thus, when she began reading, she was not prepared to surrender herself to the author and allow him to control her memory of certain fictional events. Instead, she was obviously reading with the book and the characters within it already so firmly named that she was oblivious to what was actually there. Wakefield does not know what *Charly* and *Sam* mean, because she has not read them. She has merely told herself a story about them while reading the words on the pages.

How else can we explain the gross misreading of the lines she quotes (dishonestly calling them "random samplings," when there is no such thing as random selection of such a quote as this)?

> "Sam, do I intimidate you?"
>
> "A little. The trouble with us is we're equal. Mission, college, work—I don't have an edge on you in anything."
>
> "That threatens you?"
>
> "A woman is supposed to—"
>
> "Not compete with men?" she suggested.
>
> "No, she can compete—it's just that she—"
>
> "Shouldn't do better than men."
>
> "Well, not exactly," I stammered. "You see, a woman has a certain role—"
>
> "Being mediocre?"
>
> "No, she can excel in certain areas."

"Making the bed, washing the dishes?" (From *Sam,* [Salt Lake City: Deseret Book Co., 1981], p. 83.)

Wakefield stopped the dialogue after the second speech. Even the section she quoted was pretty clear, but a reading of the whole scene makes it plain that Weyland the implied author (as opposed to Sam the narrator) is giving all the good lines to the woman. The subject gets too hot for Sam to handle when Lara says, "Okay then, don't ask me to do less than my best in my job" (*Sam,* p. 84). Lara has eloquently handled her arguments; Sam has been written as inept and confused in his. Anyone reading this scene fairly will see that if anything it is a statement *for* equal treatment of the sexes, though in fact it is not a statement at all, but rather the experience of Sam's trying to learn to cope with a woman who refuses to fit into his preconceptions. It is ironic that Wakefield accuses Jack Weyland of offering "troublingly conventional and insensitive" sexist images, when in fact, if she were not so lost in her own detached reading of the novel, she might have considered that Weyland was demonstrating precisely what Howe called a requirement of "good writing": the "ability to look at prevailing cultural myths with skepticism and objectivity." Indeed, the scene is far less stereotyped than Wakefield's assumption that books like this are largely read by "teen-age girls."

Wakefield finds Weyland's long stretches of dialogue tedious. This is not surprising—since she has removed herself from the possibility of caring about the characters, she will hardly be interested in hearing them converse.

Wakefield absurdly links these novels with gothic romance, though the primary effect of gothics is suspense and fear, which are absent from Weyland's work, and the only similarity is a male-female love interest, which is also present in a few other genres, including that of academic-literary fiction.

Wakefield wants more introspection and complexities of insight, as though Homer, Boccaccio, and Dickens should kneel at the shrine of Henry James and Virginia Woolf.

Wakefield likes to harp on the fact that the novel is predictable—"expected romance," "cliche," "formula"—yet in fact Weyland is almost always refreshingly free of cliche and unusually natural in his dialogue and characterization. The Mormon reading public has not taken Weyland to their hearts because he writes Sunday School sermons, but because he does not. When his work first appeared in the *New Era*, readers recognized at once that here was a writer who knew how real people talked, who would actually show problems that bishops didn't solve with an epigram. Wakefield started with the common literary elitist assumption that anything the masses enjoy must, a priori, be cliche-ridden and oversimplified. Not surprisingly, that is what she found.

But it is not because these views of Wakefield's are *wrong* that I reject them. They are her personal response, and she is entitled to every bias, every misreading, every absurd conclusion she desires—just as I cling to my own biases, misreadings, and absurd conclusions. Private readings of stories are inevitable and desirable. We all edit unconsciously as we read, recreating in our memories a new novel, using the written text as the base. What disturbs me about Wakefield's review is not her misreading, not her bigoted and unfair approach to the book, but the fact that she, like so many others, has not realized that currently fashionable literary theory is not only an invalid standard against which to measure Mormon literature, but is positively inimical to Mormonism and Mormon writing.

The school of critical thought that teaches readers to think rather than feel and insists that writers make intellectual statements through their fiction rather than tell tales of human experience is largely premised upon T. E. Hulme's distinction between "Classicism" and "Romanticism." For Hulme, Classicism is, in religious terms, the affirmation of the utter separateness of the human and the divine, while Romanticism's chief failing is that it supposes that man is capable of perfection. "The main thing with which [Romanticism] can be reproached is that it blurs the clear outlines of human relations . . . by introducing in them the *Perfection* that properly belongs to the non-human." What Hulme hates worst is Croce's—and, I submit, Joseph Smith's—doctrine of "*infinite progress and the infinite perfectibility of man*." In the Classical attitude, however, "Perfection is not . . . introduced on the plane of human things. It is the closing of all the roads [to human perfection], this realisation of the *tragic* significance of life, which makes it legitimate to call all other attitudes shallow." (Hulme, "Humanism and the Religious Attitude," *Speculations*, ed. Herbert Read [New York: Harcourt, Brace, Jovanovich, 1924], pp. 10-11, 17, 34, italics in original.)

The message of fiction, according to most post-Hulmian critical theory, should be that man is fallen, corrupt, imperfect, miserable, and incapable of joy for more than a few moments of epiphanic apprehension of the ever-unreachable divine. Most fiction does not in fact say this, but when critics have to cope with a great work that does not they always reinterpret it to fit the theory. Fortunately, they don't have to deal with *popular* works. The very fact that popular writing is accessible to a larger community is proof enough that it is not good and can be dismissed. For only the elect can perceive the truly divine; only the fit audience is worthy to understand the great works. Dispassionate distance is a goal, for it keeps things from getting muddy; obscurity is a virtue, for it shrinks the audience; contempt for life is the theme, for it forces us to look away from ourselves to find divinity; and soon the sacred text becomes the object of worship. Worship, mind you, *not* real reading, for we are forbidden to "naively" identify with characters, or judge a work on the basis of our emotional response (fie, the pathetic fallacy!), or suggest that a work is judged, not by absolute, mathematically perfect standards, but on the ever-changing basis of what it actually *does* to a human being who reads it.

The result has been that literary criticism can no more cope with America than with Mormonism. The most important novel of the century, in terms of actually affecting people's lives, is unquestionably Margaret Mitchell's *Gone with the Wind*, the most-read American novel of our time. But by its nature, *Gone with the Wind* is not a fit subject for this critical method. Its meaning cannot be detached and restated, except perhaps as the puerile statement, "Even when all is lost, we can survive if we go on struggling," or "Don't look for happiness out of your reach, for it is really already in your hand." Critics *do* sum up popular novels in just that fashion, completely missing the point that it is not the *meaning* that real readers look for, but rather the powerful and truthful experience. To Depression-era readers, *Gone with the Wind* was indisputably important and true. It ennobled their own struggles and taught them who they were, not in neat discourse, but in powerful and well-focused experience. Jack Weyland's books also name us to ourselves, and thousands of Mormons have found the books to be important and true to them *as Mormons*—a far more plausible measure of what is "Mormon literature" than those Wakefield seems to prefer.

For Wakefield has bought a critical theory that depends on a view of mankind that is inimical to Mormon belief. It is the point on which we differ with all of "Christianity," the point that makes us stand outside the Western tradition: We espouse the Pelagian heresy, we believe in the perfectibility of mankind, we believe that the divine can only be found in the human shape, we believe in progress. Mormon literature—that is, the stories we tell ourselves about ourselves—cannot be good literature by the standards of the literary community today, because to be "good literature" our stories must show Mormons facing "dilemmas of the soul" without resolving them. A book that shows happiness in this life, that shows reconciliation and joy, is invariably dismissed as "naive" and "simply too obvious." Jack Weyland writes of redeemable, perfectible, happy, competent people—and the reader who is a captive of literary fashion says, "Bosh—this is unrealistic."

This is not to say that Weyland is "right" and Wakefield "wrong." In fact I find *Charly* and *Sam* to be not as satisfying and believable to me as Weyland's shorter work. Wakefield has a perfect right to detest any book she likes, as long as she admits that her response stems from her personal taste and not some inherent failing in the work itself—and therefore in the poor fools who go in droves to the bookstore to buy it. Indeed, the elitist view of popular work that assumes that whatever the masses like is contemptible ignores the truth: The best-read best-seller is read by only a small fraction of the population. The number of people who read *at all* is so small that it is already elite. And those who read for the story rather than the discourse are absolutely unforgiving critics. They have no ax to grind. They never pretend to like a book they hate because it is a "great book."

Beyond the question of elitism, however, is the fact that to dismiss Weyland's work with misreading and contempt because it does not meet the literary standards of an anti-Mormon philosophy is to refuse to admit a Mormon literature at all. After all, English literature reached its peak with the most popular playwright of his time; Defoe, Dickens, and Twain forced their way into the literary canon out of the love of common people. What Hulme despises as "Romantic" writing is precisely that writing which affirms the fundamental tenets of Mormonism: that mankind is literally the offspring of God, capable of maturing into perfect beings.

We will not find great Mormon literature by finding that literature which best imitates the literature of America, any more than great English literature was found among the translations from Ovid, Horace, and Boethius. Great Mormon literature will be that literature which feels true and right to Mormon readers, for by that literature we will name ourselves. Setting out to write "great Mormon literature" is the surest way I can think of for a writer to produce trash. Jack Weyland is not a "Mormon Shakespeare." Jack Weyland is the Mormon Jack Weyland, and instead of imagining that we know what Mormon writing ought to be and condemning Mormon writers for not producing it, we might better spend our time looking at what Mormon writing *is* and discovering from it who we are.

Walking the Tightrope

From *Sunstone* magazine, April 1989

We were so smug, we Westerners, we Christians, we Mormons, when the Muslim world convulsed and bled over a mere book, a splash of words, a fillip of decorative art. People died in a riot in Pakistan—and for what? Because they thought our embassy bookstore was selling *The Satanic Verses*, a work of fiction, a *novel*. And then the Ayatollah Khomeini pronounced a death sentence on the author and urged Muslims to carry out the sentence as privateers, with a reward guaranteed.

Outrageous, disgusting—we, the civilized West, would never act that way.

Fear and Loathing in Zion

Then my mother sent me a clipping from a Utah paper, telling how Ed Firmage, noted Utah Democrat and grandson of Hugh B. Brown, had provoked outrage by asserting that his fond wish was to see four blacks among the General Authorities of the LDS church—three of them women. Just to make sure we Mormons, at least, could not pass ourselves off as wholly civilized, many volunteers in the Mormon community had made anonymous phone calls to the Firmages, many of them with veiled and not-so-veiled death threats. "You can be removed," they said.

Apparently there are some followers of the Ayatollah among the Saints.

These events happened to be juxtaposed with general conference, in which two speakers addressed the issue of critical voices within the Church. Bishop Glenn Pace's talk stated that criticism of the Church from within was the most dangerous kind. Immediately afterward Elder Dallin Oaks urged us to be extremely selective in choosing to participate in the various unofficial "alternate voices."

And then a friend sent me a clipping of Eugene England's protest on BYU's policy of discouraging its faculty from publishing in *Dialogue* and this very magazine.

This coincidence suggested to me that two continuously overlapping groups within the Church—the hierarchy and the intelligentsia—are in the process of tearing themselves into rival camps. The very division is a monstrous deformation of the way the Church is meant to function—indeed, Elder Oaks's talk can and should be read as a careful but heartfelt attempt to keep that rift from widening.

I could imagine the reactions of many of my friends—many of *you* who read this magazine, I believe. Applause for Eugene England's spirited defense of alternate LDS magazines; a slow burn as Elder Pace warned against criticism of the Church by Church members; a certain wariness throughout Elder Oaks's talk; instant solidarity with Ed Firmage in his victimization by the pinheads of Mormondom.

Through it all, I imagine many LDS intellectuals feeling that the Church hierarchy was overreacting or, worse, that it was becoming repressive and dictatorial toward legitimate free expression. Feeling, in other words, that the Church hierarchy was, on its own initiative, clamping down on all non-official voices within the Church.

There is another way of looking at this, however. A truer

way. Those among us who feel injured or oppressed by the hierarchy's policies and attitudes must remember that the finger of blame points both ways.

Perhaps the easiest and clearest way to understand our own situation is to look at what happened in the cultural and religious community of Islam.

Good Guys and Bad Guys

I watched with a mixture of gratification and embarrassment as every writers organization in America expressed its solidarity with Salman Rushdie, the man whose book, *The Satanic Verses*, led to the Ayatollah Khomeini's pronouncing a death sentence upon him.

I was gratified because I also am afraid whenever words are answered by violence; we who live by words are always vulnerable to those who have the power of the sword.

I was embarrassed, however, because in the process of defending the freedom of the press, most failed to notice that Rushdie was an unworthy champion—that defending Rushdie's freedom of the press should have been just as unpleasant to people of goodwill as defending, say, Larry Flynt's freedom to publish pornography.

Just because Khomeini behaved in a very bad way toward Rushdie did not make Rushdie one of the good guys. Quite the contrary. Rushdie is a bad guy in this story, and we defend him only because of the inappropriateness of the Ayatollah's response, not because what Rushdie did was good or even innocuous.

Assault on Faith

The Satanic Verses is a despicable book that could not have been written by a person who wished to behave decently and responsibly. The book is clearly aimed at Muslim readers; it is hard to imagine a non-Muslim reading it with anything more than mild curiosity. Yet Rushdie, as a lapsed Muslim, also knew that the Muslim audience would be outraged by it. He could only have written it as a calculated offense against his own community.

The most dangerous aspect of the literary world's knee-jerk defense of *The Satanic Verses* was the widespread assumption that because the book was fiction, it was absurd for anyone to be so angry at it. Especially galling was this frequent bit of illogic: "How dare these people get upset about *The Satanic Verses* when they haven't even read it!" This makes as much sense as saying, "How dare these people get upset about drunk drivers when they've never been run over by one!"

Storytelling does not operate in a vacuum. It fulfills a vital human need—that's why there's no human society without it and precious little human contact that does not take the form of storytelling. We can hardly get through the day without many stories of many kinds. And fiction is one of the most powerful kinds. Unlike "true" stories (history, science, news, gossip), fiction is not subject to immediate revision upon discovery of a new fact. The author of a fictional tale has absolute authority, within the world of the story, over the most fundamental area of human thought: causality, why things happen.

What happens in fiction resonates or clashes with the deepest parts of our identity: our sense of how the world works, of what it means to be human, and of who, as individuals and members of a community, we *are*. When we read fiction we either reaffirm or redefine our conception of reality to a degree surpassed by only one other type of story: religious revelation. And when fiction moves into a realm of mind where revelation holds sway, it will be the profoundest challenge to—or affirmation of—faith.

Muslims' very existence as a people depends on the holiness of Mohammed and the validity of his revelation from God. Their understanding of the way the world works depends on this. When Rushdie treated Mohammed with scorn and depicted him in a vulgar, low way, he challenged the foundation of their collective and individual identities. He tore at the very heart of who they are.

The Satanic Verses is not "pure" artistic expression. (There is no such thing, anyway.) It was anti-Islamic literature—a story by a former insider who deliberately struck at the very heart of the Islamic faith.

Anti-Mormon Literature

I remember my first exposure to hardcore anti-Mormon literature. I was in Brazil on my mission when a member brought us some pamphlets that a friend of his had been given. (You know the pattern—nobody talks to the guy about religion in his whole life, but the minute they find out he's attending Mormon meetings, they have all kinds of "information" about the Mormons.)

As I read the pamphlets, I never felt my faith challenged—I never was tempted to doubt. It was all silly stuff that I'd heard about before. But I found myself getting deeply angry because I imagined other people reading this stuff and thinking it was true. I wanted to go out and find every copy of those pamphlets and include with each one my own detailed refutation of every lie they told.

Yet that was impossible. So I found myself filled with helpless, impotent rage at how these people were creating a false image of Mormonism. They were defining for many people what the name *Mormon* stands for; they were defining the most powerful of the communities that comprise my identity; therefore they were defining *me*. I seethed for days, even after I carefully and patiently answered the questions these pamphlets had raised in the minds of the members and nonmembers I knew who had read them. It still hurts to remember—for even though my *faith* is unchallenged by them, my public identity is profoundly challenged.

Those pamphlets were written by avowed anti-Mormons. People of reason and goodwill are usually repelled by such hate literature, and sometimes are even sympathetic to the victims of such obvious lies. But what about attacks on a community written by *members*?

Back to Rushdie. Remember that countless Western authors have written about Islam in a negative or demeaning way, with few or no repercussions. Muslims might resent such writing, might try to refute it, but as long as everyone knows that the negative stories are being told by outsiders, they pose no particular threat to the epic of Islam—the more anti-Islamic they are, the less credibility they have.

But Rushdie was *not* an outsider. Rushdie might have lost his faith, he might be living in a Western nation, but to Muslims these matters are irrelevant—he wrote as a member of the Muslim community. He knew all the buttons to push. He knew all the ways to offend. And he used them.

Enemies of the Kingdom?

We don't have to go far to find a Mormon parallel. I quote from Sonia Johnson's own account in *From Housewife to Heretic* of a key moment in her Church court:

> Here is the direct quote from the transcript of the videotape [of her speech to NOW members in Kalispell, Montana]: "The leaders of the Mormon Church are somewhat isolated in Utah. Those who are directing this anti-ERA activity need a taste of the consequences of their behavior, and one of the things everyone can do is write and call church headquarters and say, 'I am outraged that the Mormons are working against my equal civil rights, and if your missionaries ever come to my door, I wouldn't consider letting them in.'" (Doubleday, 1981, p. 332.)

Johnson, as an insider, knew what pressure would be felt most by the Church. And because it was a Church member who was urging NOW members to proclaim a boycott of LDS missionaries, she had infinitely more authority than an outsider. How could this be anti-Mormonism, when a Mormon suggested it? The moment Johnson made this statement, however, she declared herself to have a higher allegiance than her allegiance to the Church. Any Mormon who gives greater priority to a non-Mormon cause than to LDS missionary work is not a Mormon at all. Johnson's excommunication was a formality—she was already gone. Most Saints knew this at once. She was beyond the pale.

But Johnson didn't see it that way. Indeed, she even claims that her suggestion to non-Mormon NOW members was a perfectly legitimate thing for a Mormon to do:

> "That's political lobbying, pure and simple," I pleaded vainly with my prosecutor-judge and his cohorts. "Lobbying is deal-making: you have something I want, I have something

> you want. Let's make a deal. The church wants women to join the church, women want the church to unhand the ERA. Women should therefore say, 'If you'll listen to us, we'll listen to you.' That's political." (Johnson, *From Housewife to Heretic,* pp. 332-33.)

Here is the root of Johnson's apostasy; here is the attitude that led her out of the Church. She believed that revelation was negotiable.

Most Mormons easily accept the idea that revelation is *responsive*—that is, that revelation comes at times when it is needed. Most of the revelations in the Doctrine and Covenants were given in response to requests, questions, or calamities. Most Mormons also accept the idea that revelation is *not universal*—that many decisions or attitudes of bishops or stake presidents or even General Authorities are merely their own best judgment, and not the literal word of God; and almost all of us are suspicious of people who claim that every thought that enters their heads comes from God.

But what Mormons *can't* accept is the idea that revelations might come as a bargain, a compromise, a deal with some pressure group. Sonia Johnson was attempting coercion—*forcing* the Church to comply with her program. Much the same thing was done by the federal government during the polygamy era; but at least none of the federal officials trying to force LDS compliance with anti-polygamy laws pretended to be members.

The root of Johnson's heresy was contempt for the principle of revelation and the living prophets, seers, and revelators who are called to govern the Lord's church. That same spirit of contempt, that same urge to pressure the Brethren into doing what can only be accomplished by prayer, is still with us.

Transforming the Church

Open, public criticism of a Church doctrine or policy, especially from within the Church, is the single least effective way to change that doctrine or policy. All that such critics succeed in doing is demonstrating that they do not believe that the Lord gives revelation to guide the prophets, and that fact declares these critics to be enemies of the fundamental point of LDS faith: that God speaks to living prophets.

Please note: It is not necessarily their *ideas* that make these critics seem to be enemies of the faith, but rather the fact that they seem to believe that Church leaders can be negotiated with like politicians. It makes these critics at once infuriating to Church members and ineffective with Church leaders. It is exactly that attitude on the part of some *Dialogue* and *Sunstone* writers that has made these magazines seem like enemies of the faith to most Mormons who are aware that they exist—because so many writers for these publications are not members of the community of believers, and some are genuine enemies of the faith. They plainly don't believe in revelation; and if they don't believe in revelation, it is difficult to understand how they are Mormons in any sense but the cultural.

Such critics sound to many Mormons the way Rushdie sounded to many Muslims; they strike at the heart of the Saints' identity, their community, their worldview, and, as Elder Pace said, they are the most dangerous storytellers in the Church, because many nonmembers—and some members—will believe that it is possible to be a Latter-day Saint and have no belief in revelation or respect for prophets, seers, and revelators.

The Possibility of Influence

Does this mean that there is no way for members to influence the Church? Does this mean that ideas can only flow from the top down? Of course not. Anyone who knows anything about Church government knows that the flow of ideas on doctrine and policy is omnidirectional. As often as not, revelation at the highest levels consists of getting ratification from the Lord for ideas first proposed and tried out in stakes, in wards, or in the minds and hearts of humble Saints. Most of the Brethren, far from being aloof declarers of the word, are passionate, involved listeners, eventually aware of every voice that is raised. And anyone who wants to be part of this vast network of teaching and discovery and transformation *can* be.

How is it done? It's so simple. No power or influence can or should be maintained in the kingdom of God except by:

Persuasion. No public ultimatums or threats, no "negotiations," but rather privately offering a new idea with a desire that the other person receive it.

Long-suffering. Not giving up because our idea seems to be rejected at first. People change, and the idea that astonished them when they first heard it becomes sweeter to them over time.

Gentleness. Never using stridency, anger, or ridicule toward those we hope to influence.

Meekness. Always being willing to obey, even when your ideas aren't accepted.

Love unfeigned. Not merely pretending to support and sustain fellow Saints, but actually loving them, desiring their happiness, trusting their goodwill.

Kindness. Never using our words to injure another, or even to return an injury we have received.

Pure knowledge. Seeking our own confirmation from the Holy Ghost before we presume to teach others, instead of immediately trusting in our own "neat ideas" or the teachings of the world.

Few of us have a calling that allows us to reprove anybody—and even fewer of us are ever moved upon by the Holy Ghost to do so. However, sometimes our ideas will seem to others to be a rebuke, and therefore we must be sure that we show them an increase in love, *lest they esteem us to be their enemy*.

The Saints will not listen to an enemy. Why should they? But they *will* listen to people who are demonstrably loyal, believing Saints. You can have far more influence in the Church if you *never* utter a word of criticism, but instead teach your values positively, in circumstances that affirm faith in the gospel and commitment to the Church. If the Saints—particularly the Church leaders—know that your "faithfulness is stronger than the cords of death," they will learn to trust that your stories are told out of "charity toward the household of faith." Then their confidence in you will strengthen, and your righteous influence in the Church will increase.

Higher Allegiances

I can imagine some of you thinking, How wimpy, how weak—has he no commitment to telling the truth?

Well, "telling the truth" is a much overrated virtue in America today. It is the all-purpose excuse for verbal cruelty and domination. How many of you would find much virtue in parents who said to their child, "You were the least talented person on that stage. It was excruciating to watch you." Or, "I always thought you were dumb, but this much stupidity surprises even me." Or, "Face it, you're deeply ugly and no amount of makeup is going to change that." All these statements might be true; but *saying* them to a person who will be deeply hurt by them is not virtuous. The noble course is to maintain a discreet silence, gently teaching the child to overcome, avoid, or live with his or her shortcomings.

Shouldn't we love the Church as good parents love their children? Shouldn't we be as gentle and careful in sharing our scant wisdom with them as we hope they will be in teaching us from their great wellsprings of wisdom? And if, like children, they sometimes stingingly reject what we offer, shouldn't we be patient, our commitment to the Church unwavering? Instead of being outraged when they read *Sunstone* and *Dialogue*, shouldn't Latter-day Saints who open these pages be fed? Isn't it worth keeping silence about some "truths" in order to earn their trust in the far more important truth that we have vowed to help them bear their burdens?

If *Sunstone* and *Dialogue* are forums for people who have left the community of believers and now scorn it, or people who have succumbed to their sins and hate the Church for not pretending their weakness is acceptable, or people who have embraced heresy and wish to proselytize for it, then how can *Sunstone* and *Dialogue* hope to be taken seriously—by Mormons—as journals of *Mormon* thought? These people may need a magazine of their own, but if *Sunstone* or *Dialogue* choose to be that magazine, no one should complain if people with positions of trust in the Church are expected not to contribute to them.

Does this mean that I think *Sunstone* and *Dialogue* should only publish items that could clear Correlation Review? Of course not. Between official publications and heresy there is a vast area for serious speculation and passionate discussion. Many—perhaps most—of the articles in these magazines fall within this vital range.

Furthermore, even if all *Sunstone* and *Dialogue* writers spoke exactly the way I have suggested, there would still be some Saints, in or out of the hierarchy, who would resent, object to, even attack these publications. A well-meant, careful statement by a loyal Saint can still be misinterpreted. And *no* work can survive a hostile reading. I've had my own tastes of this—from the Mormon Left as often as from the Mormon Right. So have many of you.

For instance, my novel *Saints* was written as an attempt to create a positive, accurate impression of early Mormonism in the minds of nonmember readers. It was important to me that nothing in the book suggest that Joseph Smith was not a prophet—but also that nothing in the book require nonmember readers to decide whether to believe that he *was* a prophet. I carefully walked the narrow line between my faith and the nonmember readers' unbelief, in the effort to give the unconverted an understanding of the lives of believers. In the process, I also wanted to give Mormon readers as real and powerful an experience of their own forebears' lives as I could.

For many thousands of readers I succeeded—but I am well aware that to some I gave great offense. I regret that offense; I would undo it if I could. I don't believe that because I am an artist I am immune from the responsibilities of Church membership; I don't have a higher allegiance to art than to the Church. Quite the opposite. I can't possibly be a *good* artist unless my highest allegiance is to the kingdom of God. Evil art, well-wrought, is all the more harmful; good art, clumsily executed, is better. Best of all, though, is good art well-made, and that's what I strive for.

When any in the Mormon audience, after a fair reading, find that I have not achieved it, I hope they will forgive my personal imperfection and trust me to grow out of it, as they also expect the rest of us to forgive their imperfections. That someone will take offense is almost inevitable whenever we make any kind of statement that rises above blandness. It will certainly happen with *Sunstone* and *Dialogue* despite the best intentions; it happens all the time to General Authorities, too. Anyone's words and acts can be misinterpreted; anyone can, through ignorance or carelessness, offend unintentionally.

Fortunately, Mormons believe it is the road to heaven, not to hell, that is paved with good intentions. We forgive each other for unintended harm.

Prophets and Assimilationists

From *Sunstone* magazine, February 1989

A recent issue of *Sunstone* reported on some negative reactions to Boyd K. Packer's address on funerals. The gist of those reactions was that General Authorities have no business meddling in areas that General Authorities don't usually meddle in.

"It isn't that he spoke about funerals," they seem to be saying. "What bothers us is that he demanded we change the way we do things. Worse yet, his changes would give the Church more control over our lives."

Indeed, if there is one theme that runs throughout Elder Packer's career as a prophet, seer, and revelator, it is this: He persists in speaking about topics that few others are willing to touch, and he persists in trying to get us to change our customs in ways that would make us even more different from the world around us than we already are. He expects us to transform ourselves as a people, and he insists on his authority to teach us how to do it.

Let me give you an extended example. Years ago, I sat in

the large BYU audience that listened as Boyd K. Packer gave his address on Mormon art. At first I was excited—what other General Authority had given art in the Church more than a passing mention?

But soon excitement gave way to dismay. Did he really propose that Eliza R. Snow's and Orson Whitney's tacky little poems be treated as seriously as truly *great* literature?

And when he made his joke about temperamental artists being "more temper than mental" I was offended. He might be an Apostle, but what did he know about artists? What did he know about art?

Years went by. I stopped dabbling in writing and made it my career. I went on to graduate school at two universities and began to make some discoveries about the world of literature in America.

At first inadvertently, but later by design, I did most of my storytelling within the genre of science fiction and fantasy. It is the one genre that allows a storyteller to create worlds that function by different rules; I needed that possibility of strangeness, that control over milieu, in order to tell the stories that seemed most important and true to me.

Science fiction and fantasy are, together, the latest incarnation of the oldest tradition in literature. From Gilgamesh and Odysseus on through medieval romances and the folktales that every community in the world adapts to its own needs, the stories that people have loved and retold all contain strangeness, the possibility of magic, the immanence of powers normally beyond the reach of human beings. My conception of the working of the world was formed primarily by Joseph Smith, and I found it impossible to tell my most truthful stories without strangeness, without the immanence of power.

But my professors, with rare exceptions, despised science fiction and fantasy. I quickly learned that they also did not understand it, did not even know how to read it. I, however, *did* know how to read and understand the works that *they* valued, and I soon discovered that at the heart of every one of their most treasured stories there was a seed of strangeness. But this tiny shred of romance was so buried in details of realism, so camouflaged by flamboyant and distracting style, that it could only be extracted with patient labor. Rarely was it worth the effort.

Why did they insist on telling their stories in disguise? Why did they despise and deplore stories that offered themselves plainly? Their stories had gained nothing and lost much. Their audience, and therefore their ability to influence the world, was small and shrinking.

But there *was* compensation for the litterateurs, a metastory that they valued more than the stories of their purported literature: the story that said, "People who can read *serious* literature are finer, more intelligent, and more important than people who read that easy stuff." Their fiction, by its very inaccessibility to untrained readers, made them an elite.

They have captured the American university English departments, and from that bastion they try—and often succeed—in their effort to make people ashamed of reading any story that is told plainly enough to be understood by an untrained reader. You know how we apologize for the stories we love: "Oh, I just read these romances / mysteries / fantasies for escape." Or, "I only read this sort of thing at the beach / on the plane / when I'm sick."

The academic-literary establishment teaches students to value only those stories that must be carefully explicated and decoded by those ordained to the high priesthood of literature. They have persuaded most Americans that any story that does not require their mediation is trash.

All the arguments and conflicts within the academic-literary establishment are simply efforts to rise higher within their hierarchy. For instance, all the obfuscation of the deconstructionists can be boiled down to a few clear concepts; but by masking their ideas in a daunting, untranslatable, circular, self-referential vocabulary, the deconstructionists have been able to pose as an even higher priesthood—Gnostics who pretend to know a Mystery, which gives them power over those who don't know the proper incantations. It is a mass of confusion, designed not to be understood.

I looked at the critical theories of the academic-literary establishment and realized that, with a few exceptions, they were worthless, good only for decoding a certain narrow group of stories. Their theories were incompetent to explain the workings of most of the stories throughout all ages of the world—so they dismissed those stories as not worth reading.

But I saw that every human society in all of history creates and devours stories as their one indispensable crop; we don't contemplate our stories, we *use* them as surely as our bodies use food. Any theory of criticism that excludes the very stories that most people love best is worthless. And any story designed to satisfy the requirements of that worthless theory would have no meaning to most people. "Serious literature" in America is devoted to creating junk food. It may be served on fine china, but it's still a Twinkie, and after fifty years it's getting pretty stale.

It isn't just literature. *Every* American art except film has walked down that same road. Young painters and sculptors are taught to despise art that an untrained audience might love. Young musicians are taught to compose music that is deliberately unmelodic and unrhythmic and inaccessible. Young poets are encouraged to believe that clear communication is the enemy, not the essence, of their art.

The result is that young artists who study at American universities and believe what they are taught come away incapable of having any effect on the American people at large. Their art is valued only by a jaded audience that is generally incapable of being moved or transformed except at the shallowest level, which is the same as saying that their art is wasted.

When I finally understood this, I remembered Boyd K. Packer's address to the students and faculty in the arts at BYU. Though his rhetoric was sometimes offensive and his examples perhaps unhelpful, his fundamental message was not only true but the most important thing that Mormon artists could learn: The artistic standards of the world are directly inimical, not only to the Church, but also to art itself.

Many who resented Elder Packer's address said that he wanted to turn our art into propaganda for the Church. This is absurd. He was warning us that we were turning our art into propaganda for worldly elitists. He was warning us that if we believed their lies, we would be incapable of producing art that had any value whatsoever. And he was right. He was also ignored—not by all, but by far too many. BYU's English department too often prides itself on its ability to persuade its student writers to accept the values of the academic-literary establishment. BYU's music department still rewards most those young composers whose music has the least power to move an untrained audience. Only the art and theatre departments occasionally give honor to students and faculty who create works that might have some effect on an audience of volunteers. All these years after Elder Packer's address, BYU still does not take him very seriously.

To put it plainly, Elder Packer was warning Mormon artists of the danger of assimilationism. Assimilationism is the greatest danger facing the Church in America. There is enormous pressure for us to conform to the values of the nation around us. We have weakened under that pressure, and there is grave danger that it will destroy us, not by breaking the Church apart, but by erasing the boundary between the Church and the world. The Great Apostasy did not come because members left the Church; it came when the Church adopted the values, philosophies, and practices of the world.

As to Elder Packer's recent speech about funerals, it is astonishing that anyone could imagine that it is somehow inappropriate for an Apostle to insist on the Church's close involvement with the rituals surrounding death. Putting the bishop in charge of the funeral services does not take control away from the family. The bishop—who knows the family well—is more likely to respond to the desires of the family and the needs of the religious community in which they live than the paid stranger who is usually in charge. At every Mormon funeral I've attended, the family spends most of its time fulfilling the expectations of the undertaker. Do we give greater authority to the American mortician than to the Mormon bishop?

Too often the answer is yes. Yet Elder Packer has not forgotten that Mormonism is a revolutionary movement, that it is our job to subvert or overthrow the world's institutions and philosophies. He reminds us that the gospel touches every part of life, that the Spirit of God cannot be shunted into a small compartment and remain alive in us. He has dared to think and speak about how the Saints must change in order to better fit the gospel.

He is most often criticized by those who prefer to change gospel ideals and customs until it is possible to be a "Mormon" without ever having to go through the embarrassment of being different from the non-Mormons they admire. These assimilationists long to reconcile the world and the Church by changing the Church to fit the world.

If we refuse to let an Apostle teach us how we should deal with death, if we refuse to let an Apostle teach us how we should conceive and use our art, then in what sense do we sustain him as an Apostle? And if, having rejected that Apostle, we turn to undertakers and anti-religious elitists to teach us on those same subjects, then in what sense do we remain Latter-day Saints?

Assimilationists excuse themselves by whimpering, "Surely there's nothing wrong with learning truth from many sources. After all, even the Apostles sometimes disagree." But they rarely consider and choose between the teachings of Apostles; rather they seize on any apostolic statement that seems to justify their adherence to the views of the world. The assimilationists invariably *act* on the assumption that the world knows better than the Church.

Sonia Johnson trusted in the doctrines of feminism more than she valued her fellowship with the Saints; her excommunication only formalized her shift in loyalties from the community of Jesus Christ to a competing one.

The businessmen who erect their obscene mansions on the hills of Salt Lake and Utah valleys trust in their money more than they value their solemn commitment to live consecrated lives; they struggle to resist fellowship with the faithful poor, forgetting that wealth, not poverty, is the fatal disease of the world.

The professors who teach their students not to create art for the masses trust in the academic-literary establishment more than they value the struggle to bring to pass the eternal life of man; the students who believe them are effectively silenced for life in a world that is hungry for their voices.

Parents who teach their children not to date or marry good and faithful Saints of another race trust in the opinions of their bigoted neighbors more than they value Christ's commandment that we be one.

Knowing that these values are contrary to the gospel, many of these assimilationists seek to distort the gospel and deceive the rest of us into thinking it supports the degenerate values they have learned from the world. If they ever succeed, then we, the Church, the salt of the earth, will have lost our savor.

The Church as a community is far from perfect, but its imperfection comes from its failure to live up to the ideals of the gospel, not from the few areas where we have succeeded in differentiating ourselves from the world. The status quo within the Church is not very good, but the status quo outside it is much worse. The Church is in need of transformation, but the true revolutionaries within the Church are those who are radically orthodox, not those who are loudly assimilationist. When Elder Packer says something that makes the assimilationists squeal, it is safe to assume he is doing his proper work as a prophet.

Science Fiction and the Mormon Religion

A 1985 letter to the editor of *Dialogue,* responding to an article by Michael Collings

I'd like to add a lengthy footnote to Michael R. Collings's "Refracted Visions and Future Worlds: Mormonism and Science Fiction" (*Dialogue* 17 [Autumn 1984]: 107-16).

Collings is at his best talking about how non-Mormon writers have dealt with Mormonism in science fiction; I'd like to point out a book that was published after Collings wrote his article: *Them Bones* by Howard Waldrop (Ace, 1984). This novel, part of Terry Carr's new Ace Specials series of science fiction novels, is a wonderful tongue-in-cheek action-packed time travel story, the sort of sense-of-wonder tale that is at the heart of the sf genre.

Mormons will especially take note of the way Waldrop uses Mormonism in a delightful "bootstrap" paradox. In the bootstrap paradox, which was given its most powerful expression in Heinlein's "By His Bootstraps" and "All You Zombies," a character goes back into the past and sets in motion a chain of events that ultimately leads back to himself. For instance, in "All You Zombies," Heinlein gives us a character who, through time travel and a sex-change operation, is her own father and mother—an entirely self-existing, uncreated person. The same thing is done with a watch in the movie *Somewhere in Time*—one character received it as a gift from the other, then went back in time and gave it to her. At no point was the watch manufactured; it could not exist. Utterly impossible, but lots of fun.

In Waldrop's *Them Bones*, Colonel Spaulding, the commander of an expedition that has gone back in time to try to change the future, was born and raised a Mormon. Waldrop gets a few things wrong—does any Mormon ever call our meetings "services"?—but as ancient Indians keep killing off his expedition one by one, he becomes obsessed with the Book of Mormon. Whereupon he copies it over on metal plates and wanders off, presumably to go bury it in a hillside in upstate New York. It's hard to imagine many people besides Mormons getting the paradox—that the Book of Mormon caused its own creation—or even the joke about the Book of Mormon being a "Spaulding" manuscript after all. So we'll have to consider this a freebie that fun-loving Howard Waldrop has tossed in to delight his Mormon friends (and outrage a few who won't realize that this is all done in sport).

In "Refracted Visions," Collings does touch upon, but doesn't resolve, the question of how a Mormon writing science fiction should deal with religion. While George Scithers's proscription of mentions of God and angels in science fiction is about as silly as most of the rest of the things George Scithers says, it still reflects, superficially, the stance that science fiction inevitably takes: radical realism. Science fiction stories must take place within a mechanistic cause-and-effect system—or seem to. Thus, while God and Christ are rather often characters in science fiction, they are always explained away. Most recently this is done in Barry Malzberg's fine story "Quartermain" (*Isaac Asimov's Science Fiction Magazine*, January 1985), where Jesus' life is reenacted (or enacted in the first place?) by an obsessive role-player who just can't seem to leave well enough alone. In other science fiction stories, God usually turns out to be an alien (e.g., Arthur Clarke's *Childhood's End*) or a machine or—you get the idea.

So what does a Latter-day Saint do when entering this radically realistic genre?

Since only a handful of us have done it, and at present I'm the most-published Mormon in the genre, it seems most pertinent for me to mention what *I* have done. I resolved long ago, when I was a playwright trying not to lose more than a few thousand dollars a year writing plays for the Mormon audience, that I would never attempt to use my writing to overtly preach the gospel in my "literary" works. That is, when I wrote for the *Ensign*, I of course wrote openly and favorably about Mormonism. But in my plays, the question of faith did not come up. If characters believed, then that was fine; if they didn't, then fine; but I found boring and usually offensive the endless plays about people wrestling with their faith. The sappy plays always ended with conversion. The artsy plays always ended with desperate doubt. So what? It was (and is) my belief that most people who suppose they are struggling for faith are in fact struggling with far deeper and less intellectually available desires; and those who actually have faith do not bother with questions about what they *believe* that they believe. Faith exists in actions, not in emotions; I speak more about my characters and to my audience in what I make my characters *do* than in what I have them say or think.

Furthermore, I believe that I present Mormon theology most eloquently when I do not speak *about* it at all. I believe it is impossible for a writer to intellectually control his or her works at the most fundamental level: the most powerful effects of a work emerge from those decisions that the writer did not know he or she was making, for the decision simply felt inevitable, because it was right and true, not to be questioned or examined. In short, every human being's true faith is contained in what it does not occur to us to question.

So when Collings notices "generalized analogues" to Mormonism in my books *Capitol* and *The Worthing Chronicle*, he is actually noticing things that I did not deliberately do. On a conscious level, *Worthing* was an exploration of layers of storytelling, dreams within tales within memories; but I am not surprised that most LDS sf readers who have discussed the book with me have declared that they could tell all the way through that I was a Mormon. As long as I don't interfere with my own storytelling, I suspect that my works will always reveal my beliefs, both orthodox and unwitting heretical. And I believe that such expressions of faith, unconsciously placed within a story, are the most honest and also most powerful messages a writer can give; they are, in essence, the expression of the author's conceived universe, and the reader who believes and cares about the story will dwell, for a time, in the author's world and receive powerful vicarious memories that become part of the reader's own.

Naturally, with this point of view I found the Glen Larson approach both silly and offensive; I also find that most Mormon critics who have commented on my work and Larson's make the same self-contradictory mistake: They find Larson's approach—dropping in trivial LDS references—superficial, and then complain that because I don't do the same, I am denying/concealing/ ignoring my Mormonism.

Truth is, LDS theology is every bit as radically realistic as science fiction; if Joseph Smith and the rest of us in our subsequent collective theological evolution have done anything, we have explained godhood in a completely rational way. In the process, however, we Mormons have completely abandoned mechanistic causation and adopted final, or purposive, causation: The universe acts the way it does because it *wants* to, say we. The result is that my writing is received in some sf circles as particularly powerful, with a surprising and yet comfortable worldview; while many others (a majority of those who care at all) are disturbed, annoyed, or threatened by the religion in my writing even though religion is almost never openly discussed. They are uncomfortable in my fictional universe because it forces the believing reader to accept a causal system that makes every human being completely responsible for his own actions. This is directly contrary to the prevailing Calvinist literary mode, which holds that human beings have no particular free will, but rather respond uncomfortably as Life (not God, who is out of fashion) dangles them like spiders over a fire, sustaining them as long as he feels like it, dropping them when he gets bored. They have become, in other words, uncomfortable with the notion of purpose, free will, and personal responsibility, which LDS theology uniquely proposes.

So LDS readers who natter about the violence in my stories, or the homosexuality in exactly one of my hundred-odd published or performed works, or my failure to "bear my testimony" in *Saints*, are in effect asking me to deal with the most fundamental matters in a shallow, trivial, obvious, and inevitably ineffective way, all the while not noticing that I am already dealing with the LDS cosmology—or my version of it—in everything I do; but on an unconscious level that I discover only after the work is finished. I have come to trust that it will always be present in every work that I write with honesty and passion—which is, I believe, all of them.

However, if there are those who would prefer to see Mormon sf writers deal with something that "is recognizably religious and thematically 'Mormon,'" then I can mention a story I just completed, called "Salvage," which will appear sometime in the next year or so in one publication or another. It deals with Mormons overtly because it is set in a future Utah; the main character is a non-Mormon who discovers the community of faith only by realizing that he does not belong to it. It is, I am told, a very religious story, and I see that now; when I wrote it, it was simply a tale about a small-time expedition to try to salvage legendary hidden gold from the Salt Lake Temple, which is half-submerged in the rising waters of the Mormon Sea (a reborn Lake Bonneville).

I will be interested to see what a thoughtful writer like Collings will think of it, though I expect I'll hear much more from the lunatic fringe that believes that a Mormon writer who does not fulfill their personal agenda is somehow corrupt. The fact remains, though, that the story itself dealt with Mormonism only tangentially. Except for my wife, Kristine, no Latter-day Saint has yet read the story. Yet all who have read it have found it very religious, though perfectly compatible with the rationalist requirements of science fiction. So, apparently, it can be done, at least to the satisfaction of non-Mormons. As to satisfying Mormons—well, Mark 6:4 addressed that.

Addendum

In the years since this letter was written, my story "Salvage" appeared in *The Magazine of Fantasy and Science Fiction* and is now part of my collection of explicitly LDS science fiction stories, *The Folk of the Fringe*. I have launched my series of science fiction novels based on the Book of Mormon, and my novels that retell, in allegorical form, the life of Joseph Smith.

More important, I have been joined as a Mormon writing science fiction for the general audience by several talented writers who have achieved significant works within the field. Shayne Bell and Virginia Baker are both deserving winners of the Writers of the Future contest, and Shayne's novel *Nicoji* is an extraordinarily fine debut novel. I think neither Bell nor Baker would dispute me, however, in noting Dave Wolverton as the foremost of the new Mormon science fiction writers. With three novels—*On My Way to Paradise, Serpent Catch,* and *Path of the Hero*—Wolverton sets high standards for intelligent and emotionally powerful fiction, regardless of genre. LDS readers will also notice with delight how Wolverton wrestles with and explores vital themes in LDS theology and religion; other LDS readers will be astonished to realize that it is possible for an LDS writer to be even more "offensive" than me! I hope, however, that having read the essays on Mormon art in this book, you will be able, not to look *past* the sexual candor of some of Wolverton's writing, but rather to look *through* it to see what he is saying about human nature and the consequences of human desire. And as more LDS writers join me, Wolverton, Bell, and Baker in offering stories to the world, I can't help but think that we are doing our part to help brighten the Light of Christ in many hearts and minds.

PART FOUR

Building Zion

What is Zion? It is the happiest place and the happiest people on Earth.

How do we get there? We don't. We have to turn our own community into that place.

How do we do it? We must all try to make *others* as happy as we can. The paradox is that only by willingly sacrificing our own desires for the genuine good of others can we then find happiness for ourselves.

What are the limitations? We can only do for others what is within our power to do; we cannot always know what is good for them and will truly make them happy; and we cannot give gifts to others that they refuse to receive.

Zion will only be achieved, then, by a people who are very strict with themselves and yet whose rules are designed to give happiness and freedom to those who follow them. No human being is wise enough to devise such perfect rules alone; that is why Zion, when it is created again, will use the laws given to us for our happiness by the Lord. But in Zion, we will never lose sight of the purpose of the laws; we will never follow them blindly in circumstances where enforcing them would defeat their own purpose. The laws of God are firm in principle and flexible in application. The letter kills, but the spirit gives life. We are utterly rigorous with ourselves in applying these laws, and as forgiving as possible with others.

Still, while Zion is obliged to admit any who are willing to agree to live by its laws, it is not obliged to tolerate those who wish to have the benefits of the good community without fulfilling their responsibilities. Lapses, repented of, must be forgiven; questions, proposals, arguments, and outright dissent must be listened to and accommodated wherever possible. But Zion need not and should not allow those who would destroy it to remain within the community. Ultimately, those who cannot be happy within Zion—which usually means those too undisciplined to live the law or so determined to control others that they cannot tolerate any variance from their vision of correct behavior—must always be offered the option, and at times given no choice but, to leave.

It is a delicate, difficult balance, which is why we do not put our faith in men or women to devise our rules. At the same time, we must rely on men and women to lead us in our collective endeavors; we must trust each other, and at times those given that trust will fail us. Tolerance of well-meaning error must be part of the life of Zion, along with forgiveness of deliberate error later repented of. Section 121 of the Doctrine and Covenants explains the only kind of power and authority that can possibly be consistent with Zion; and the only ones who cannot lead in Zion are those who refuse to abide by that greatest of social covenants.

As a science fiction writer I have wrestled in book after book, story after story, with the question of what makes a good community, of how the individual and the community must balance each other's rights and needs. Someday I hope to reach some firm and final answers. Here, though, are the best and clearest thoughts I have reached along the way.

Consecration: A Law We Can Live With

A Parable

A man awoke one morning hearing the words of a dream, and when he wrote them down he discovered that they were the words that the chronicler of the Book of Mormon might have written, had he lived in our time, setting down a record of our dealings with each other and with the Lord:

1. And it came to pass in the latter days that most of the believers in the promised land had set their hearts upon the things of the world.

2. They labored all day and into the night, both men and women, to earn money to buy the things the world called good, or to rise to a position of great honor in the world.

3. But the money they earned was never enough, and the things they bought did not make them happy, and the offices and honors they won were never secure:

4. Even when they had earned great wealth, the world persuaded them that they needed more,

5. And even when they had achieved high offices and great honors, their ambition was unsatisfied,

6. For they had forgotten that the rewards of the world come from Satan, and so have no substance.

7. To win the rewards of the world, they sacrificed the time they should have spent teaching their children.

8. They thrust their little ones out of their home into the care of strangers, in order to earn enough money to buy a grand house.

9. And when they had their grand house, the world said, They must be great people to have such a house!

10. But their children were strangers in their new house; they knew neither their father nor their mother, and often left the place, as a traveler leaves an unfriendly inn without a backward glance.

11. And again, they showered their children with presents: they gave them fine clothing, and let them ride through the streets in splendid vehicles,

12. And taught them to despise those whose clothing was plain, and mock those who rode in old cars, and jeer at those who had to walk because they had no car at all.

13. Thus they taught their children to persecute the poor, and to set their hearts upon the pleasures of the world.

14. And yet when these children took expensive poisons of ecstasy, and broke the laws of chastity, and cast aside other laws of God as things of no worth,

15. Their parents blamed the Church for failing them, or the school for corrupting their values.

16. They did not see that their children had learned the main lesson of their parents' lives:

17. That any sacrifice is acceptable in order to win the rewards of the world,

18. Even the sacrifice of their own children.

19. These Saints who served the world more than the Lord gathered themselves in neighborhoods of costly houses, high on the hill so that all could see their splendor.

20. Thus they formed congregations of the rich, for the poor could not afford to live among them; this was an abomination in the sight of the Lord.

21. They paid their tithes and offerings and called themselves righteous,

22. Yet they forbade their children to befriend the children of men and women who labored with their hands, who earned little money, or who were despised by the world.

23. And when they remembered the poor—those who lived in small houses, with many children sleeping in each room—they said to themselves,

24. If only these people had not sinned, the Lord would have blessed them as we have been blessed;

25. Or, If only these people had learned to restrain themselves, they would not have so many children and so they would not be so poor;

26. Or, If only these people had educated themselves, they would be wise enough to live better than this, as we are;

27. Or, If only these people would work harder, they would not have to live in such poverty.

28. And many of the poor, hearing these things, believed them, and despised themselves even more than the rich despised them, and all their dreams and longings were for the rewards of the world, and they turned away their hearts from righteousness.

29. Thus the world had led away the believers to the worship of Mammon; yet the believers imagined themselves to be righteous because they attended their meetings and paid their tithes.

30. And the Lord looked upon them and said, Where is the people who will be ready to receive me at my coming?

31. Where is the people who are good to the needy,

32. Who honor men and women for their works and not for their possessions,

33. For their wisdom and not their worldly education,

34. For their righteousness and not their vain display?

35. Yea, the Lord looked out upon his church and said, Where is Zion?

36. Have I not given them prophets and teachers, doctrine and covenants?

37. Why then do they seek the honors of the world?

38. Why then do they steal from the poor, and then say that the Lord has blessed them?

39. For all things belong to me, saith the Lord, and all who labor righteously, with all their might, are worthy of an equal share of the bounty of the land;

40. Therefore any man who takes more than he needs, and does not give his surplus to the bishop to share it with the poor, has taken that which I have not given him;
41. Verily, verily, saith the Lord unto that man, you will have what you have stolen for a little season, but you will have no joy in it,
42. And at the last day you will stand with those who have no reward, because you did not share with the humblest of my brethren, and so you have no part in their inheritance.
43. The wicked world has nothing of itself, so whatever the world bestows is stolen property.
44. If the world gives you much, then you must give away much,
45. For that which you keep will be lost, and only as much as you give away can you keep forever.
46. What is Zion? said the Lord, Yea, where is the people ready to receive me at my coming?

And when the man had written down the words of his dream, he trembled in fear, for he knew that he was guilty. He said to his wife, "If the Lord sent an angel to gather the people of Zion, would he come to us, here in our fine house, with all our possessions? I fear that our house is a fortress we have built to keep the Lord out of our lives."

To his surprise, his wife suddenly wept. "Oh, my husband!" she said. "I have had a dream every night for a week, but I was ashamed to tell you. In my dream we were about to buy a new Mercedes. We gave the money to the salesman, but when he handed us the keys to the car they burned our hands, and we couldn't hold them.

"So we took back the money and went to the bishop, and said, 'We were going to buy a Mercedes, but the keys burn our hands. So instead we'll buy a cheaper car that is only as much as we need. Here's the rest of the money; because we were going to spend it on vanity, we know that it's more than we need. Therefore it's our surplus; give it to the poor and needy. Also, here is the title to our old car; give it to someone who needs it.'

"And in my dream the bishop said, 'I was praying for help, because yesterday I saw the bishop of another ward weeping because his ward is very poor, and though his people work hard, they never have enough money to make ends meet. He told me that there was a worthy young woman in his ward who couldn't go to college because of her family's poverty. He told me that there were children in his ward whose parents could never take them to the doctor, because they had no money to pay. He told me of families with no table to eat on, of children with no books to read, of single mothers who were bowed down with weariness and grief because they worked all day to feed their children and had no time to teach them righteousness. And I told that bishop, It can't be right for your people to have so little, and my people to have so much. I'll pray for the Lord to soften the hearts of the members of my ward, so they'll turn their hearts with compassion toward the poor. And now here you are, and I can go to that bishop and tell him that he can pay the tuition of that worthy girl, and take those children to the doctor, and buy the furniture and the books and even the freedom that many of the people in his ward need so badly. Now look what great blessings we can share with the humblest of the Saints. And as for your old car, I know where it must also go.'"

"What a wonderful dream," said the man.

"But it isn't finished," said his wife. "In my dream we went to church several weeks later, and as we got out of our modest new car, we saw the wealthiest man in the ward drive into the parking lot. He was driving our old car.

"And in my dream we both became angry that the bishop gave our car, not to the poor, but to this rich old man who had all he needed in the world. We went to the bishop and said, 'We didn't give you this car so you could share it with the rich!'

"And then the bishop put his arms around our shoulders and said, 'Oh, my dear brother, my dear sister, I must have made a mistake. I thought you gave that car to the Lord's church, to be used for righteous purposes. I thought that I was the one called to be the judge in Zion, to decide who should be steward over the Lord's property. Instead I see that you still own that car in your hearts. So I'll give you back the title; it wasn't part of your surplus after all.'

"Then we were ashamed, and you said, 'Bishop, we should have trusted you. Keep the car.' And I also said to him, 'Bishop, keep the car, and forgive us for meddling.'

"He smiled at us, and said, 'Let me tell you what you don't know. That rich old man also came to me, as you did, and gave me all his surplus to use as the Lord saw fit. He told me that he had even sold his cars, because, being retired, he could take the bus or walk to do everything he needed to do. But I said, "No you can't. You need a car because I need you to bring four elderly widows to church every Sunday." And he said, "What can I do? I've already sold my cars." That was when I gave him the title to your old car. He's using it in the service of the Lord.'

"And then we realized that the bishop had fulfilled his stewardship, and we apologized for mistrusting him. And he said, 'Your problem wasn't that you didn't trust me. Your problem was that you still thought of the car as yours.'

"But I said, 'No, Bishop. Our problem was that our car still owned us. It still had the power to turn us away from good works. It isn't enough to give our surplus to the bishop. We have to change our hearts so that we no longer covet the things we own. Even what we still have belongs to the Lord. We're stewards; we have no property of our own.'"

Her husband shouted aloud when he heard the end of her dream. "Now I understand the parable of the talents. Now I know the real sin of the unrighteous servant, the one who buried the one talent in the ground. He was treating the money as if it belonged to *him,* withholding it from anyone else, so that it couldn't be used for anything. But the other servants, knowing that the money *didn't* belong to them, put it out with moneylenders so that it could be used to build things, to make things. Everyone profited—the servants who shared freely, the moneylenders, and the people who borrowed and then repaid. But the one who clung to his money and let no one else use it—no one benefited, not even him. And his constant fear of losing that money became a burden to him. It was his soul he buried in the ground, his freedom."

Then both the husband and the wife knew that their dreams were wise ones. And from that day forward they ceased to own any thing or to be owned by any thing. Many things were still recorded as their property, after the manner of the world, but whatever they had, they shared freely with any who needed it. Thus they had no fear of being robbed, for they owned nothing. They no longer cared about impressing their wealthy and educated friends, and soon they learned which of their old friends were true, and which of them were false, because the true friends rejoiced with them in their new freedom, while the false friends mocked and despised them.

And then something happened that surprised them most of all. Because they no longer cared about the world's measurement of a person's worth, they began to see other members of the Church in a new light. They began to see past clothing or manners or grammar or education and made new friends among the very people they had once looked down on. They learned that there was far more wisdom and goodness among the humble people of the Church than they had ever found among the wealthy and sophisticated. They had once ridiculed these people because they had "bad taste"; now they understood that "good taste" was completely unrelated to goodness of heart.

A year after their dreams they lived in a more modest home, and their children had learned to live without many luxuries, and most of their old friends spoke of them with the same sort of mournfulness that they used when speaking of the dead. "How they've come down in the world," said their old friends, their voices full of pity and scorn.

Yet this man and woman, these dreamers, had found true brotherhood and sisterhood, true fellowship with the Saints, because for the first time in their lives they did not allow the world's corrupt values to make a division between them and other Saints. They truly believed that all their possessions belonged to the Lord and, through him, to all God's children; and so they used the money the world gave them to bless others. By the world's standards they had moved downward in social class. By the Lord's standards they had finally become full partakers in the work and the glory of the Lord.

And they were not alone. For many people had received the same dreams, had come to yearn for the same freedom and goodness. And when the chronicler wrote the scriptural account of that time, it ended like this:

46. Where is Zion? said the Lord, Yea, where is the people ready to receive me at my coming?

47. And the people of the Church heard his voice, and repented.

48. They repented of their covetousness, and they brought their surplus to the Lord.

49. Those who had large houses gave them to those who had large families;

50. They were not ashamed to go down and live in small houses among the laborers and the poor.

51. And their children learned to despise the rewards of the world, and instead valued the rewards of the spirit, and so the rising generation was pure in heart, and not corrupted.

52. The bishops of the Church were astonished at the great wealth that suddenly poured into their storehouses,

53. And they sent forth the money gathered in America so it could bless Saints all over the world, helping feed and clothe and educate a righteous generation.

54. And when the Saints discovered that all their brothers and sisters had their rightful portions of the wealth of the world, and none were hungry or naked or homeless, none were untrained or uneducated, and none were afraid or ashamed, they asked each other,

55. How did this happen? What made us change?

56. Then they realized that nothing had compelled them to change;

57. The Lord had given them no new commandment;

58. The Spirit of God had only invited them to live more fully the law they already had, and they answered with the righteous yearning of their own hearts.

59. Thus they became an ensign to all nations, for although none of them had wealth as the world measured it, they all had enough,

60. And that is the one thing which the covetous world can never have.

Eugene England and the Lighted Lamp

A review of Eugene England's *Why the Church Is As True As the Gospel* (Bookcraft, 1986)

I can't read Eugene England's personal essays as a critic. I am too much a part of the natural audience for his words. I can't step outside and dispassionately watch his transaction with his readers. I am caught up, captured, possessed, and for a time I see the world through his eyes.

Later, after reflection, I can report on the experience. That is as close to "criticism" as I can come. It is perhaps the only sort of criticism appropriate for such essays. For Eugene England's commitment to the Church, his truthfulness of vision, his simple clarity of expression defy criticism by any detached standard. In fact, England implicitly denies the virtue of detachment. If your whole self is not involved in what he has to say, then he is not speaking to you at all; and if he is not speaking to you, then you have real cause for self-doubt, for he is speaking to all men and women of good heart.

So what you will read here is not an analysis; at times it may not seem to be "about" England's book at all. It is instead what reading England's words made me want to say, not to him, but to fellow members of his intended audience.

Hugh Nibley wrote the foreword to Eugene England's book—an apt choice, since England is the first writer to merit serious consideration as heir to Hugh Nibley's hitherto unique place in the Church. Years ago, on my mission, I was captivated by Hugh Nibley's essay on priests and prophets. (I have not reread it since, so my memory of it is shaped by what I wanted to hear then and what I have needed to remember since.) He told the story of the Old Testament prophet who came into the city from the wilderness. That prophet was not part of the hierarchy of priests, whose charge was the maintenance of the status quo. He came to shake things up, to cry repentance, to change the life of the people, bring them closer to their covenant with the Lord.

At the time, I thought, Yes, that's what the Church needs. The title of "prophet" has been co-opted by the hierarchy. We need people to stir us up, to cry repentance to the complacent. And because I had this thought during my adolescence, I naturally considered myself a perfect candidate for such a lonely but valuable job. I will stand outside and be a gadfly, thought I.

That is a role that so many of us who have intellectual or artistic gifts choose to take. And yet it is exactly the opposite of the true prophetic role. The outsider is never capable of reforming those inside the community. For why should those who are committed to the community pay the slightest attention to the advice of those who have no such commitment? And if no one listens to you, of what use are your well-meant criticisms?

Bad enough are the "murmurings" of those within the community, poisoning the air, making the community less cooperative, fragmenting it, breaking it apart. Good leaders in every community, including the Church, spend most of their time healing those inner fractures—plugging the leaks in the dam, so to speak. When we think we see bishops or Apostles, Relief Society presidents or mission presidents trying to force Church members to be absolute conformists, to make the Church uniform, made up of ranks and rows of marching morons, what is really going on (most of the time) is an attempt to heal breaches, to give the community strength and integrity, to help it continue to exist across space and time instead of crumbling into unconnected individuals. They are trying to keep the Church, our most important community, alive.

Yet at least the murmurers and grumblers and bickerers and snipers are inside the community. When we (we intellectuals, scholars, and artists, we who have ingested great dollops of the wisdom of the world) take a pose outside the Church, speaking as if our distance gave us greater perspective, we have crossed the river, taken the elevator, rented a room, and now lean out the windows of the great and spacious building, jeering at those who are trying to guide others to take hold of the Iron Rod.

Because, you see, the distinction between people who hold to the Iron Rod and people who follow the Liahona is spurious. The Iron Rod *is* the Liahona; the Liahona *is* the Iron Rod. They both work by faith. The Iron Rod is useless unless you hold to it, follow it; you only do so if you believe it leads somewhere good, and want to go where it leads. The Liahona tells you nothing unless you have exactly the kind of obedient faith that is typified by holding to the Iron Rod. The true Liahona will never prompt anyone to let go of the Iron Rod and wander unconnected through the fog. If you have a Liahona that suggests otherwise, throw it away. It's a counterfeit.

You cannot understand a community if you do not live as a committed member of it. Outsiders—even neutral or sympathetic ones, like anthropologists, sociologists, psychologists, theologians who try to understand what Mormonism is, what Mormons are—always embarrass themselves when they draw conclusions from their observations. For observing the words and actions of the Saints tells little about what those words and actions mean: their cause and purpose, and the degree of importance the Saints give to them. From the outside the Church looks monolithic; from the inside we see how hard it is to make a coherent community out of the myriad purposes and opinions and concerns and needs of the Saints.

Communities, after all, exist only as they are believed in by the members of the community—they are creatures of faith. The Church is what we believe it to be, and what we believe it to be directs our behavior within the community of Saints. The very fact of your committed participation in the community changes it to some degree; the very fact of your committed participation also changes you. Only in that synthesis of self and community does the individual acquire any power to change the Church; only in that synthesis does the Church acquire any power to change the individual. That is what I misunderstood in reading Nibley's essay and thinking that it justified my foolish idea of believing in the gospel without participating in the Church. The prophets of the Old Testament were not members of the hierarchy in their day, but they *were* members of the community. They came from the wilderness into the city preaching the same gospel and the same God that the priests in the temple served and worshipped. No matter how angry people might become at some of the things they said, those who met them, who heard their words, could not doubt that they belonged. They were members. They spoke to Israel from within Israel.

Christ went to the temple to teach, not because that's where the crowds were—he gathered crowds quite nicely without seeking them out—but because he was a committed member of a temple-centered community. He affirmed the truthfulness of the law and the prophets even as he transformed the people's understanding of them; he demanded more, not less rigorous obedience to the fundamental law.

I have learned over the years that the Spirit never speaks to me when I ask for blessings for myself. Guidance in those times always comes from someone else—from my wife, my bishop, a teacher, a book. But when I am participating in the Church, and a member needs something that I cannot provide yet which must be provided, then the Spirit will sometimes answer that member's prayer or need or hope through me. It is only as we serve each other in righteousness that Christ can act through us; and unless we are engaged in the works of Christ through the Church, which is the body of Christ in the world, becoming together his hands and his feet, his ears and his mouth, so that his will is enacted through our actions, his mind spoken through our words, then all our wisdom, our learning, our intelligence are like a tree that puts forth neither leaves nor fruit. Not only will it give no benefit to anyone else; such a tree is also doomed to die.

Which brings me back, at last, to Eugene England and his book of essays. The title essay, "Why the Church Is As True As the Gospel," explicitly expresses this commitment to the community of Saints. England is walking the narrow path on which our feet are also set, he is holding firmly to the Iron Rod to which we also cling, and because of that his words of encouragement and chastisement, of insight and illumination, all have meaning to us. We know that what he describes we will also see as we progress along the path to the tree; and if we have already passed through the experience he describes, we recognize that he is speaking truthfully if not always perfectly, and he helps us make new sense of and gain greater strength from those events in our past.

Eugene England, then, like Hugh Nibley before him, is actually fulfilling that prophet-role that is not available to heads of the hierarchy, for *their* ordination as Prophets, Seers, and Revelators perforce redefines those three words and those three roles. However much their minds may wander in seeking new understanding, in puzzling out the billion questions yet unanswered, the billion sights as yet unseeable by our present feeble light (which is, even so, the brightest light of understanding available in the world), their position at the head of the Church makes it impossible or undesirable for them to speak of those wonderings and speculations. They understand too clearly the price the Church has paid in the past when that limitation on the hierarchy was not understood and observed—when Brigham Young spoke his speculations on the role of Adam, when John Taylor expressed his conviction that the loss of polygamy would mean the apostasy of the Church, when a twentieth-century Apostle uttered his tentative ideas about a relationship between lineage and the degrees of glory in the afterlife, when another twentieth-century Apostle published his speculations about the future role of blacks in the Church as if they were Mormon doctrine. Because every word of a General Authority is seized upon, magnified, distorted, and then broadcast willy-nilly through the Church, causing tremors and upheavals in the community of the Saints, they must weigh their words carefully, or, in some cases, cause harm because they do not weigh their words carefully enough. Their position of authority gives them great power to influence and bind together the community, but that power must be used delicately, for it can cause division and fragmentation, confusion and weakness.

All their words and acts are confined by the needs of the Church; because these men are the center, they must hold firm, they are not free to fly, not in public at least, not where others will mistake their personal speculations for firm doctrine. They must speak the fundamental truths that will make us one, yet when they attempt to elaborate on them they run the grave risk of obscuring them.

This is why the Church needs Hugh Nibley and Eugene England. They are not invested with official authority, so that the only authority they have in their writing is its truthfulness, the resonance of their ideas in the hearts of their readers. They have the freedom to be sincerely wrong without disrupting the community of Saints. Where the leaders of the Church must, as servants of the host, prepare the wedding feast and keep all in order, a Nibley or an England can, without harm, carry a lamp of his own to the wedding, bringing a gift of light to all who partake of the feast.

I approached *Why the Church Is As True As the Gospel* already disposed to agree with the title essay; some of you may be more skeptical. What struck me most forcefully, however, was that most of the other essays bore out the truth of his title essay. That is, his best and most valuable insights could only have been spoken by someone who sees the world from the perspective of a committed member of the Church. I have read other works by LDS writers of great intellectual gifts who misunderstood what matters and tried to see the Church from the perspective of the world's intellectual elite; their analysis was sometimes impressive, but it meant nothing, since it could not be translated into good action. England's analysis, on the other hand, is sometimes unsatisfying, but when translated into action, it is invariably good, leading to Good. That makes England's essays worth writing, worth reading, and a valid part of the upbuilding of the kingdom of God. This is a consecrated book, even if it is not always correct.

Two essays in *Why the Church Is As True As the Gospel* do not follow this pattern. "Shakespeare and the At Onement of Jesus Christ" and "Hawthorne and the Virtue of Sin" are not written to fellow Saints, but rather to fellow scholars of literature. Though they are infused with England's faith, these two essays are a clear contrast with the rest of the book, and however interesting they are as an intellectual exercise, however I would love to have been surprised by them in a scholarly journal, they are futile by comparison with the other essays in the book. If they were all he wrote, England would merely be a Mormon intellectual, of which the Church already has an oversupply, considering that the need for them is so very small. England is at his best—as are all teachers at all times—telling stories, rather than explaining someone else's stories.

For Eugene England is not a Mormon intellectual. To call him that is to deny the value of his work. His life is not the servant of his mind; his mind is the servant of his life. He is a Saint whose abilities are consecrated to the building up of the kingdom of God. Among those abilities are intellect and language, but there is no hint in his writing that he esteems them any higher than other abilities that he or other Saints might have. The head does not say to the hand, I have no need of thee; England neither has nor supports the notion that the "life of the mind" is a valid goal for the Latter-day Saint. If you long for someone to tell you that your unconnection with the Church is the result of your superiority, that you cannot fully participate in the Church because of your artistic sensitivity or intellectual discipline, you will find no comfort from Eugene England. Implicit in his writing is the truth that life without full participation in the Church is not life at all. Implicit also is the truth that full participation in the Church does not require or even reward the abandonment of intellect. The true Saint hungers for greater light and knowledge, and greater light and knowledge cannot be had apart from participation in the community of Saints.

So England's book cannot be read safely. You cannot receive even a portion of the value of this book if you do not put yourself at risk in the reading of it, if you are not willing to be changed. But if you place yourself in his hands and receive his words with an open, undefended heart, he will bring you closer to the Spirit of God and closer to the community of Saints. That, and that alone, is the work worth doing.

The Hypocrites of Homosexuality

From *Sunstone* magazine, February 1990

When I was an undergraduate theatre student, I was aware, and not happily so, how pervasive was the reach of the underculture of homosexuality among my friends and acquaintances. After a while I stopped being shocked to discover that someone I had known well, or whose talent I admired, was either moving into or already a part of the not-so-clandestine network of gay relationships. I learned that being homosexual does not destroy a person's talent or deny those aspects of their character that I had already come to love and admire. I did learn that for most of them their highest allegiance was to their membership in the community that gave them access to sex. As a not-particularly-pure-minded heterosexual adolescent, I understood the intensity of sexual desire; as a student of human communities, I have since come to understand how character is shaped by—or surrendered to—one's allegiances.

One thing is certain: one cannot serve two masters. And when one's life is given over to one community that demands utter allegiance, it cannot be given to another. The LDS church is one such community. The homosexual community seems to be another. And when I read the statements of those who claim to be both LDS and homosexual, trying to persuade the former community to cease making their membership contingent upon abandoning the latter, I wonder if they realize that the price of such "tolerance" would be, in the long run, the destruction of the Church.

We Latter-day Saints know that we are eternal beings who must gain control of our bodies and direct our lives toward the good of others in order to be worthy of an adult role in the hereafter. So the regulation of sexual drives is designed not just to preserve the community of the Saints but also to improve and educate the individuals within it. The Church asks no more of its members who are tempted toward homosexuality than it does of its unmarried adolescents, its widows and widowers, its divorced members, and its members who never marry. Furthermore, the Lord even guides the sexual behavior of those who are married, expecting them to use their sexual powers responsibly and in a proportionate role within the marriage.

The argument by the hypocrites of homosexuality that homosexual tendencies are genetically ingrained in some individuals is almost laughably irrelevant. We are all genetically predisposed toward some sin or another; we are all expected to control those genetic predispositions when it is possible. It is for God to judge which individuals are tempted beyond their ability to bear or beyond their ability to resist. But it is the responsibility of the Church and the Saints never to lose sight of the goal of perfect obedience to laws designed for our happiness.

The average fifteen-year-old teenage boy is genetically predisposed to mate with random enthusiasm. We are compassionate and forgiving of those who cannot resist this temptation, but we do not regard as adult anyone who has not overcome it; and we can only help others overcome these "genetic predispositions" by teaching them that we expect them to meet a higher standard of behavior than the one their own bodies teach them. Are we somehow cruel and overdomineering when we teach young men and young women that their lives will be better and happier if they have no memory of sexual intercourse with others to deal with when they finally are married? On the contrary, we would be heartless and cruel if we did not.

The hypocrites of homosexuality are, of course, already

preparing to answer these statements by accusing me of homophobia, gay-bashing, bigotry, intolerance; but nothing that I have said here—and nothing that has been said by any of the prophets or any of the Church leaders who have dealt with this issue—can be construed as advocating, encouraging, or even allowing harsh personal treatment of individuals who are unable to resist the temptation to have sexual relations with persons of the same sex. On the contrary, the teachings of the Lord are clear in regard to the way we must deal with sinners. Christ treated them with compassion—as long as they confessed that their sin was a sin. Only when they attempted to pretend that their sin was righteousness did he harshly name them for what they were: fools, hypocrites, sinners. Hypocrites because they were unwilling to change their behavior and instead attempted to change the law to fit it; fools because they thought that deceiving an easily deceivable society would achieve the impossible goal of also deceiving God.

The Church has plenty of room for individuals who are struggling to overcome their temptation toward homosexual behavior. But for the protection of the Saints and the good of the persons themselves, the Church has no room for those who, instead of repenting of homosexuality, wish it to become an acceptable behavior in the society of the Saints. They are wolves in sheep's clothing, preaching meekness while attempting to devour the flock.

No act of violence is ever appropriate to protect Christianity from those who would rob it of its meaning. None of us is without sin—the casting of stones is not our duty or our privilege. All that must ever be done to answer them is to declare the truth, and to deny them the right to call themselves Latter-day Saints while proclaiming their false doctrine. Even as Christ freed from her accusers the woman taken in adultery, he told her, Go and sin no more.

No community can endure that does not hold its members responsible for their own actions. Being human, we try from childhood on to put the blame for the bad things we do on someone or something else. And to one degree or another, we do accept plausible excuses—enough, at least, to allow us to temper our judgment. The American polity defines the crime of second-degree murder to allow for those whose anger was greatly provoked, as distinguished from those who coldly kill for gain. Also, we are willing to alter the terms of confinement of those whose unacceptable behavior clearly derived from mental illness. In short, we recognize the principle that those who have as little control over their own behavior as small children should be treated as compassionately—yet firmly—as we treat small children.

What we do with small children is to establish clear boundaries and offer swift but mild punishment for crossing them. As their capacity to understand and obey increases, the boundaries broaden but the consequences of crossing them become more severe.

Within the Church, the young person who experiments with homosexual behavior should be counseled with, not excommunicated. But as the adolescent moves into adulthood and continues to engage in sinful practices far beyond the level of experimentation, then the consequences within the Church must grow more severe and more long-lasting; unfortunately, they may also be more public as well.

This applies also to the polity, the community of citizens at large. Laws against homosexual behavior should remain on the books, not to be indiscriminately enforced against anyone who happens to be caught violating them, but to be used when necessary to send a clear message that those who flagrantly violate society's regulation of sexual behavior cannot be permitted to remain as acceptable, equal citizens within that society.

The goal of the polity is not to put homosexuals in jail. The goal is to discourage people from engaging in homosexual practices in the first place, and, when they nevertheless proceed in their homosexual behavior, to encourage them to do so discreetly, so as not to shake the confidence of the community in the polity's ability to provide rules for safe, stable, dependable marriage and family relationships.

Those who would be members of a community must sacrifice the satisfaction of some of their individual desires in order to maintain the existence of that community. They must, in other words, obey the rules that define what that community is. Those who are not willing or able to obey the rules should honestly admit the fact and withdraw from membership.

Thus, just as America, a democratic society, is under no

obligation to preserve some imagined "right" of citizens who wish to use their freedom to overthrow that democracy and institute tyranny, so likewise the LDS church, which is founded on the idea that the word of God as revealed through his prophets should determine the behavior of the Saints, is under no obligation to protect some supposed "right" of those members who would like to persuade us that neither God nor the prophets has the authority to regulate them.

If the Church has not the authority to tell its members that they may not engage in homosexual practices, then it has no authority at all. And if we accept the argument of the hypocrites of homosexuality that their sin is not a sin, we have destroyed ourselves.

Furthermore, if we allow ourselves to be intimidated by our fear of the world's censure into silence in the face of attempts by homosexuals to make their sin acceptable under the laws of the polity, then we have abandoned our role as teachers of righteousness.

The repentant homosexual must be met with forgiveness. Even hypocritical homosexuals must be treated individually with compassion. But the collective behavior of the hypocrites of homosexuality must be met with our most forceful arguments and our complete intolerance of their lies. To act otherwise is to give more respect to the opinions of men than to the judgments of God.

Tolerance is not the fundamental virtue, to which all others must give way. The fundamental virtue is to love the Lord with all our heart, might, mind, and strength; and then to love our neighbor as ourself. Despite all the rhetoric of the hypocrites of homosexuality about how if we were true Christians, we would accept them fully without expecting them to change their behavior, we know that the Lord looks upon sin without the least degree of tolerance, and that he expects us to strive for perfection.

That we must treat sinners kindly is true; that we must courageously and firmly reject sin is also true. Those whose "kindness" causes them to wink at sin are not being kind at all, for the only hope of joy that these people have is to recognize their sin and repent of it. True kindness is to be ever courteous and warm toward individuals, while confronting them always with our rejection of any arguments justifying their self-gratification. That will earn us their love and gratitude in the day of their repentance, even if during the time they still embrace their sins they lash out at us as if we were their enemies.

And if it happens that they never repent, then in the day of their grief they cannot blame us for helping them deceive and destroy themselves. That is how we keep ourselves unspotted by the blood of this generation, even as we labor to help our brothers and sisters free themselves from the tyranny of sin.

Some Observations

I predicted toward the beginning of the preceding essay that those who have already accepted the dogmas of the homosexual community as a source of truth superior to the words of the prophets would be incapable of reading what I had actually written here and would instead interpret my words as intolerance, oppression, gay-bashing, or—an epithet used now without a shred of its original meaning—"homophobia." My prediction was exactly fulfilled, and I have had ample opportunity to observe that some supposed proponents of liberty for homosexuals do not believe in freedom of speech for anyone who disagrees with them.

This is true even within the Mormon community. For instance, Signature Books responded to publication of "The Hypocrites of Homosexuality" by suggesting to *Sunstone* magazine, where the essay appeared, that Signature might not be able to continue distributing that magazine if they continued to publish essays by me—a thinly veiled attempt to suppress my ability to get my writings published, even while Signature was still profiting from publication of my book *Saintspeak,* which I had sold to them under different editorial leadership. When I called Gary Bergera, editor of Signature Books, about his letter, he was apparently incapable of seeing that his attempt to get *Sunstone* to cease publishing my writings had anything to do with oppression. In his view, the cause of freedom requires Signature to make every effort to stop me from having a chance to speak a single word that might persuade someone that being a Latter-day Saint means trying to live by the gospel as taught by the prophets, while they insist on their own freedom to continue with their clear and relentless crusade to persuade Mormons to take currently fashionable worldly wisdom as a better source of truth than the teachings of the prophets. Fortunately, freedom of the press still prevails on both sides, and I have no fear that, given equal freedom to speak, the teachings of the prophets will continue to prevail within the Mormon community.

In fact, even outside the LDS community, it has become clearer and clearer to me, since writing this essay, that gay activism as a movement is no longer looking for civil rights, which by and large homosexuals already have. Rather they are seeking to enforce acceptance of their sexual liaisons as having equal validity with heterosexual marriages, to the point of having legal rights as spouses, the right to adopt children, and the right to insist that their behavior be taught to children in public schools as a completely acceptable "alternative lifestyle." It does not take a homophobe to recognize how destructive such a program will be in a society already reeling from the terrible consequences of "no-fault" divorce, social tolerance of extramarital promiscuity, and failing to protect our adolescents until they can channel their sexual passions in a socially productive way. Having already lost control of the car, we now find the gay activists screaming at us to speed up as we drive headlong toward the cliff.

Oddly enough, even as I am attacked by some as a homophobe, I am attacked by others as being too supportive of homosexuality, simply because I cannot see individual homosexuals, in or out of my books, as anything other than human beings with as complex a combination of good and evil in them as I find within myself. In my own view, I am walking a middle way, which condemns the sin but loves the sinner. Apparently this cannot satisfy those who either hate the sinner or love the sin; both are equally enraged by my unacceptable posture. Still, I did attempt to explain my views in the following response, first posted on *America Online*, an interactive computer service where I host an area called "The Hatrack River Town Meeting."

Recently on Prodigy's "Card, Orson Scott" topic, one participant wrote a brief message saying that it really bothered him when I made the main character of *Songmaster,* Ansset, a homosexual; the message-writer used the word *abomination* to refer to homosexuality. The responses from others online were understanding even when in firm disagreement. Several pointed out that while the character of Josif was a homosexual, the character of Ansset was not. One wrote affirming the sympathy that I obviously had for homosexuals, and warning the original letter-writer of "homophobia." I could not leave the discussion that way without a reply.

Concerning the discussion of homosexuality in *Songmaster,* I must agree with those who held that Ansset "was" not a homosexual, though he engaged (or attempted to engage) in homosexual acts. As Kinsey pointed out, most American males (and many American females), even as long ago as the 1950s, had *some* kind of same-sex sexual gratification or experience. Engaging in homosexual behavior one time does not mean that you have that as your inevitable destiny.

Science has barely scratched the surface of the question of how much of our behavior has a genetic source and how much is environmental (and of course science doesn't even admit to any other possibility—i.e., a preexistent soul or, as someone called it somewhere, an *aiua*). Even in the clearest cases of genetic causation (schizophrenia, for instance), the percentages are significant but not even close to being absolute. That is, there are many who "should" be schizophrenic and yet they are not; and even among those who have schizophrenic episodes, there are degrees of predisposition. So if we discover, eventually, that homosexuality has a genetic indicator, this does not mean that all who have the indicator are equally pushed in that direction—or even that anyone who has the desire is necessarily forced to engage in homosexual acts. The predisposition toward various behaviors does not mean that a person no longer has volition. Desire is not identical to action, at least among civilized people. After all, the desire to do physical violence is far more pervasive among human males than homosexuality, yet human males are expected to curb it except when playing hockey. Civilization depends on people being able to master those of their predispositions that are regarded as unacceptable by the community they live in.

There are communities within American culture that regard homosexuality as just another viable lifestyle, absolutely harmless and therefore no more to be shunned or censured than an inability to carry a tune (and *less* obnoxious than a predisposition toward, say, public nose-picking). There are other communities within American culture that regard homosexual acts as sins, so that good people try to control any such desires and not act them out. And there are communities that regard homosexuality as an evil which must be violently expunged.

The violent ones are themselves engaging in a far more serious anti-civilized pattern of behavior, of course, and I think there is no room in America for violence directed against any group (or any individual) for any reason short of immediate defense against physical attack—which doesn't often come up with homosexuals. But apart from the violent ones, I do think there is room within our society for people with many views of homosexuality, as well as of other non-majority behaviors. (Race and gender are not behaviors, and so what I am saying about attitudes toward homosexual behavior does not necessarily extend to attitudes toward race or gender.)

As long as we can freely leave one community and enter another, either geographically or socially, then doesn't reasonable tolerance of others' beliefs and practices allow communities that voluntarily agree to regard certain behaviors as sins as much right to their beliefs as communities that voluntarily agree to regard those same behaviors as acceptable? I find that those who plead for tolerance are far too often prone to wanting to hunt down and wipe out the last vestige of what they call intolerance—and are incapable of realizing that this behavior is, in itself, exactly as intolerant and usually as unjust as the behavior they so rigorously oppose.

All of which brings us back to my novel *Songmaster.* In dealing with Ansset, a beautiful, artistic child in the highest circles of power, the question of both pederasty and homosexuality had to be dealt with, because both would come up. I can think of few power cultures in human history where they have not! I think that may be because those who seek power tend to be inclined to self-gratification and to domination of others through sexual as well as other kinds of intercourse; and since power cultures are usually male-dominated, a beautiful but vulnerable male is going to find that most domination and exploitation come from men. There's more to it than that, I'm sure, but one thing was unavoidable: Ansset was going to be approached.

I could have used the "child molester" idea and made it a moral monster who used him—but I had other monsters using him when they trained him to be an assassin, and I had loaded them up with enough burdens in the story. Besides, I thought of the many homosexuals I had known, and while a few of them (about the normal proportion among human males) were nasty and vicious and domineering, the majority (again the normal proportion) were decent and kind and meant well in their dealings with others.

So in creating Josif, I tried to show him as a good man with desires that, in the case of Ansset, he had no intention of acting on. Neither of them set out to have a seduction scene. But Josif, for whatever reasons, looked upon men as potential sexual partners, and this was going to color his relationship with Ansset, even by avoidance, exactly as heterosexual men find that their desire for women colors their relationships even with women they do not intend to approach sexually. Ansset responded, not to his *own* sexual desires, but to Josif's unspoken need for him. And in the process, Ansset learned exactly how much he had been forced to sacrifice in order to become a Songbird. Josif, too, was treated with the viciousness that evil people too often use toward those who are really no danger to them at all; some people, when they see that someone is truly helpless, become *more* cruel (as the Rodney King videotape and the subsequent footage of rioters beating innocent passersby all demonstrated).

In all of this, I was not attempting any kind of brief either "for" or "against" homosexuality. In my own life, I live in a religious community whose entire raison d'etre is that we believe God makes his will known through prophets. Those prophets have taught us to regard homosexual behavior as a sin, along with many other desired acts, both "natural" and "un-". Just as our natural desires for heterosexual contact outside of marriage are to be curbed, we are also taught to curb homosexual desires—along with many, many others. It is not easy for any of us to control those things we desire most (though of course we always do well at controlling those desires we barely have at all).

It is quite possible for me to regard homosexuality as a temptation toward a difficult sin, much to be avoided by members of my religious community, and at the same time recognize that others feel differently about it—and that even those homosexuals within my religious community (which means most of those I have known in my life) are people of value, as they either struggle to control their desires or, despairing of that, leave the religious community that requires of them what they no longer desire to do. The only people I have contempt for are those who try to remain inside Mormonism while denying the validity of guidance from the prophets, and I oppose them, not because they live as homosexuals, but because of the hypocrisy of claiming to be Mormon while denying the only reason for the Mormon community to exist. If they prevailed, it would destroy our community. Homosexuals themselves pose no such threat, provided that those who are Mormon admit that a homosexual act is a sin as long as the prophet declares it to be so, while those who do not accept the prophet's authority refrain from pretending to be Mormon.

Given my personal feelings about the individual homosexuals I have known and, in some cases, have regarded and still regard as dear friends, and my religious beliefs about what God requires of those of us who take upon ourselves the commitment to be members of the Mormon church, it is hardly likely that *Songmaster* would be either "for" or "against" homosexuals. What the novel offers is a treatment of characters who share, between them, a forbidden act that took place because of hunger on one side, compassion on the other, and genuine love and friendship on both parts. I was not trying to show that homosexuality was "beautiful" or "natural"—in fact, sex of any kind is likely to be "beautiful" only to the participants, and it is hard to make a case for the naturalness of such an obviously counter-evolutionary trend as same-sex mating. Those issues were irrelevant. The *friendship* between Ansset and Josif was the beautiful and natural thing, even if it eventually led them on a mutually self-destructive path. And both of them were cruelly used by the society around them, being regarded as expendable or exploitable.

The only thing I would quarrel with in any of the attitudes I've seen expressed on this subject in this particular discussion on Prodigy is the use of two words: *abomination* and *homophobia*. Both are relatively meaningless these days, and are most often used to express loathing; therefore, while the loathing may be sincere, the words become less than helpful in serious discussion. In fact, in technical theological language (an oxymoron?) the act of sodomy is classed as being exactly as abominable as bestiality (note that it is the act, not the desire, we're talking about)—but that doesn't make it any more helpful to use the word in civilized discussion.

Likewise, there are people who show a virulence in their hatred of homosexuals that is obsessive, personal, and pathological, and I suppose *homophobia* could be regarded as the technical word for that. In the overwhelming majority of the cases where I've seen *homophobia* used, however, it was used not to describe the pathological condition, but rather as an ugly word to fling at anyone who does not go along with the political agenda or self-story of various activist wings of the American homosexual community. If you don't accept the full politically correct line (i.e., homosexuals can't help it and shouldn't ever be expected not to do as they like, and should be treated as martyrs and given special protection under the law), then you are a homophobe in the view of these people.

Frankly, I find that this quickly turns into a delicious hypocrisy: Those whose agenda is "tolerance" and who insist that ugly words like *faggot* not be used against them have found an exactly analogous word to use as a weapon in their virulent intolerance of those who disapprove of either their behavior or their political agenda. They use the word to silence opposition, to subvert legitimate discussion. Those who use the word this way are so convinced of the righteousness of their cause that they are willing to deny the right of others to disagree with them. Thus, in the name of tolerance of diversity, they seek to force others into a perfect uniformity of thought. The fascism of the Left is no more attractive than the fascism of the Right.

In *Songmaster* (and also in the third *Homecoming* novel, *The Ships of Earth*, the only other place where I have dealt with homosexuality in my fiction) I attempt to create real and living characters. I find it nearly impossible to create a character that I do not end up understanding and sympathizing with to some degree. Thus it should surprise no one that I treat homosexuals in my fiction with understanding and sympathy. This does not mean that I don't also regard homosexual behavior as inappropriate for those who purport to be Latter-day Saints. I see no contradiction between the two ideas; indeed, I fail to see how an uncompassionate person could *be* a good Christian, or a good Latter-day Saint in particular.

I suppose I can take some comfort from the fact that over the years I have been savaged both for showing too much sympathy for the "abomination" of homosexuality and for showing too much "homophobic" opposition to the political agenda of the radical homosexual community. If either group of intolerant extremists felt comfortable with my works and my words, I would have reason to reexamine my position. As things stand right now, however, I think I am annoying exactly the right people on both sides, and so will continue as I have in the past, to attempt to discover the truth of every aspect of human life and then to tell what truth I believe I have found, as best I can, in both my fiction and my nonfiction.

Living in Zion

A speech given at the Plotting Zion conference,
May 1990

Most utopias—or, rather, most attempts at utopias—have started from an exclusivist premise that society will work perfectly if we can just get rid of all the people who are so different that they'll make trouble. If we can just get everybody to think alike, then our new system will work perfectly. So only people who agree perfectly will be admitted to the society.

Many of these utopias, when attempted, have more or less succeeded for one generation. The trouble is that the next generation is not composed of volunteers. They weren't selected for uniformity of thought. The next generation becomes a barbarian invasion that almost always kills the utopia they were born into. The Shakers tried to get around this. By forbidding marriage and the having of children, perhaps they hoped to keep their principles pure a little longer. The trouble is, with those restrictions they couldn't get enough converts to stay alive as a community.

Breaking the One-Generation Barrier

But is that one-generation limit absolute? The Zion society that we read about in the Book of Mormon in 4 Nephi lasted for three generations. And it was *not* exclusive. They didn't isolate themselves, they included *everybody*. And it worked. So did Enoch's Zion, and perhaps Melchizedek's Salem as well, though we aren't given much of an idea about how long they lasted.

In fact, we aren't given many details at all. What scraps of scripture we have about ancient Zion say things like, "There was no poor among them." (Contrary to what some of my more business-minded friends think, that doesn't mean they *excluded* the poor. It meant they *shared* with them.) I think the best *recent* model we have of a kind of social-experiment society that became self-perpetuating and lasted for several generations before it corrupted and lost its ideals is the United States itself. No way can we call it a successful utopia in the sense that it was perfect, a Zion society, but it *did* meet its own fairly limited agenda for quite a while, before it started becoming something quite different. It did outlast the first generation.

So how can we Latter-day Saints, charged with building Zion among us, create a utopia that can cross that one-generation boundary?

I think that we have to start by realizing that Zion is *not* exclusive. The idea of Zion is *not our property*. Zion may begin with the Saints, but to succeed it cannot remain with us alone. If we don't share it, we can't have it. So Zion has to be open and tolerant of thought and speech, cultural differences, other religions, and yet also insistent on fair and right behavior toward each other so that it can last. Zion is open to all who will accept the rules of the society, who will constrain their private desires in order to make the community life peaceful and free. It may very well draw its strength from the gospel of Jesus Christ and the faith of the Saints, but it will draw its *members* from all people of goodwill; and when the world says, in fulfillment of prophecy, "Let us go up to Zion," they will find that Zion extends its love not only to the homebound child, but also to the returning prodigal; not only to the temple people, but also to the Samaritan; not only to the house of Israel, but also to the stranger, the Gentile. And not just to *desirable* immigrants bearing gifts, but also to the empty-handed. Emma Lazarus thought her poem was the voice of America, but America has long since repudiated it, if indeed it was ever really true. Rather, her poem is the voice of Zion.

> "Give me your tired, your poor,
> Your huddled masses yearning to breathe free,
> The wretched refuse of your teeming shore,
> Send these, the homeless, tempest-tossed to me,
> I lift my lamp beside the golden door."
> (From "The New Colossus.")

We Latter-day Saints have now what America once had within its reach—the light of freedom and justice; and we stand where America once stood—at the golden door of Zion. Will we go in?

No, never, if we think to go in alone. Unless we open this door to all the world, we will never pass through that door ourselves.

So when they go up to Zion seeking peace, what will these strangers find? I think what they'll find is that the earth is full—there is enough and to spare—and that they are not strangers anymore.

The first time a Latter-day Saint Zion was attempted, it was killed by the covetousness of the Saints, rich and poor alike, and by the laws of the United States. For Zion to be built in this world, both these problems must be solved. There must be a people *ready* to live the law of consecration, and there must be a polity, a governing system, able to sustain and preserve it. First, let's consider the polity—partly because I have less to say about it.

What is vital to the creation of the polity of Zion? I don't think the particular form that is chosen is all that important. There are obviously some forms that are not going to work at all, but I don't think we need to work out the details and the organizational charts of some government system. There may very well be some ideal form for the government of Zion, but we probably will not invent it before we find ourselves living it. The constitution of Zion will inevitably evolve among the people of goodwill and good judgment who are trying to work together in that common cause. The formal constitution will eventually respond to the actual one, which is the way it usually works in the world and in the Church. You all know perfectly well that in any ward or stake, regardless of what the organizational chart might say, you soon learn the network of people who actually do what they say they'll do; those are the ones you rely on, regardless of the outward form.

Trust

The persistence of any government depends from moment to moment on *trust*—the trust of the public and of individuals in those who are making the decisions. It's important even now to sustain the government of the United States and our local governments, but it will be infinitely more important when we turn our property over to the polity. We have to believe that our leaders will administer that property for the benefit of the whole, and not for their private gain. There are plenty of examples of failure in that regard. I think of labor unions which once won that kind of trust from their membership; many of them have lost that trust, squandered it. Another example is the *nomenklatura* system in the Soviet Union, which made a mockery of the principles of communism. By their constant selfish exploitation of their power, the people in power made the people they governed both cynical and covetous.

Bishops right now have, to a degree, the kind of trust that is needed—in part because of tradition, in part because of the checks and balances within the wards and stakes, and, perhaps in largest part, because of the character of the men chosen for this calling. Having collectively earned that trust, bishops are, next to mission presidents, the most individually powerful people in the Church today. It's not unbelievable, to me at least, that at this moment many Latter-day Saints might well be willing to sign over all their property to their bishop and receive back what is needful as their stewardship, because to most of us it would be unthinkable that the bishop might steal something that we consecrated. We have great trust that he'll try his best to act for the good of the people that he governs.

Now, when the bishop actually oversees all property, all industry, all commerce, all production in the polity, the current ward organization obviously must be drastically revised. We don't need as many bishops, and they must be unencumbered. Thus we see the Church's current effort to move as many responsibilities as possible *from* the bishop *to* the quorums and the Relief Society. We may not all be aware that we are doing this in preparation for bishops' assuming their role within the law of consecration, but I believe that that is the ultimate goal.

I do have one selfish worry, though, about the system in Zion. What will be the place of the artist? I search in vain in the writings of Joseph Smith. He was writing for a people that were economically readier than we are now for the kind of system he described—that is, small industry and small freeholding farmers who could turn everything over and receive back a stewardship and make it work. That pattern doesn't necessarily apply to big assembly-line factories, or, specifically in my selfish case, to what in the world you do with somebody who makes up stories for a living. Most entertainers in American society today—including people in sports and movies and television, all of the performing arts—either live hand-to-mouth, struggling just to survive, or they have an honest job and only do this other thing on the side. Only a handful "hit it big," and when they do, they are rewarded out of all proportion to any kind of contribution they make to society. It is a really lousy system. But I *can* think of a worse one, which is the way we award government grants to artists, favoring the ones who promote the interests of a narrow artistic elite that unrelentingly rewards conformity to its norms and subversion of the norms of the society at large. I envision a Zion in which freedom of speech, of creation, is well protected, where copies of art are made available freely to all who desire them, and where artists have enough time to create their works without fear of their families suffering want.

Yet at the same time, artists should not be allowed to withdraw from the society at large into an elitist community, where they would talk only to each other—they would contribute like every other citizen to the common good. The painter would take his turn at garbage collection along with the scholar, the farmer, the grocer, and the bishop. The writer would minister to the sick and care for the troubled child along with the doctor, the teacher, the governor, the fireman, the plumber, and the scientist.

Careers in Zion

But even in that list of careers, I'm ignoring what I think is one of the greatest blessings of Zion: the abolition of the whole idea of a career. In Zion no one would have to *be* one thing all their lives. While you're doing plumbing, you're a plumber—but in the mornings you may be a student and in the evenings a singer, and next year you may be a historian, and ten years from now it might be your rock carvings that many travelers stop to see as they travel from one village of Zion to another.

Imagine your whole life following such a shifting pattern. You might start out doing clerical work—I skipped the burger-flipping stage—then take ten years to teach and civilize your young children. But when they're all in school you might find that your love of gardening leads you to tend an orchard or a vineyard. That may lead you at the age of forty to the study of genetics, and from there you may spend five years of your life wrestling with the problem of curing a terrible disease; and then you'll find yourself and your spouse living in the desert, planting gardens that will raise clouds of moisture and change the climate of a devastated region; and then you'll go to a foreign land and preach the gospel for a few years and stay to serve as a teacher; and finally you'll come back home and write a book about some of your experiences, and a few hundred people will read it and love you for having written it.

And then one day someone will say to you, "Hi, nice to meet you, what do you *do*?"

What is your answer? Typist? Gardener? Farmer? Parent? Teacher? Scientist? Ecologist? Epidemiologist? Missionary? Writer?

All of those. None of them.

Here's your answer: "I do everything I'm asked to do, and able to do, and righteously desire to do."

Then maybe he'll say, "No, no. I mean, what *are* you?"

You'll be a little confused by the question and you'll say, "I'm a follower of Jesus Christ." Because that's the only answer you'll know, the only career you'll have—the only commitment to a course of action that will last your whole life.

If we abolish the concept of career, and replace it with stewardships, tasks, projects, public service, and callings, then not only will we all be better people—no longer divided into classes, no longer fawning over celebrities and elitists—but also our scientists will do better science, because they won't be hemmed into a single discipline; our historians will do better history, because they will actually have lived and worked among many groups and societies, giving them a better lens through which to view the evidence of the past; our doctors will be better healers, because their patients will not be organic bags of disease and disorder, but living souls; our teachers will be better teachers, because they will know and love the families out of which their students come; and our artists will be better artists, because instead of creating art that merely responds to what other artists have done, they will create art that speaks to the community, democratic art that is designed to communicate, as powerfully and truthfully as possible, with as many people as will look or listen.

If ten million people in Zion read and love my novel, then *my* reward is their appreciation and honor; I will still have the use of no larger proportion of the world's goods than the teacher or the plumber or the doctor—or than the writer whose story pleases only a hundred readers. The honest laborer is worthy of his penny—no more, no less. In the body of Zion, the eye does not say to the foot, you're worthless because you have no vision; rather the eye says, please carry me to where I can see new vision, and then through me we will look at it together.

Church and State

In creating Zion *here*, we're going to have to take into account two American traditions: the separation of church and state, and the relationship between business and government. I think the latter is the better model for the relationship between the church and the polity of Zion: close involvement, cooperation, yet with each restricting what the other can do; lots of people stepping back and forth, but each group ultimately making independent decisions within its sphere. We can see this, I think, most clearly if we realize that the Federal Reserve is the ultimate business authority, deliberately slow to respond to the pressures of democracy, the way the Church is slow to respond to fads and fashions of the world. When government fails to control the excesses of business, business itself suffers.

I envision the American Zion beginning with bishops handling the economy, public works, and public welfare, while elected officials handle law, defense, and public order. Overall economic strategies could be developed by elected and called officials, working together, responding carefully to the commandments of the Lord and the desires and needs of the people. And no one, ever, *ever*, would think of leadership or management as a career.

This is the way it works in the Church as it is now. I think of Joe Hamilton, the Blazer teacher in our ward who taught my son for a couple of years. A wonderful man. A great and loving teacher. He keeps telling his bishopric, "Don't release me from this. This is the best calling I've ever had." This means, I think, a little bit more if you realize that this man was stake president for ten years until two years ago. Immediately upon his release, his first calling was as Blazer teacher, and he accepted it without batting an eye. He treated that calling just as seriously as he ever treated being stake president.

A comparable example is that of Jae Ballif, a man who was in a position of great leadership and responsibility at BYU and who, without batting an eye, has stepped back to being a professor, which I think is a wonderful message to the faculty about how he values what they do.

Imagine how much better the world of business would be if it worked with jobs the same way the Church does with callings. Today's CEO might be personnel clerk tomorrow; today's assembly-line worker might be tomorrow's marketing manager—and with no sense of demotion or promotion, success or failure. It's just a different calling. You just serve where you're needed, and where your skills are more appropriate. Imagine, first of all, how much fairer the wages would be! Imagine how much better the managers would treat those who worked under their supervision. Imagine how much better those who work at the lowest levels would capture the vision of the entire organization.

For that matter, imagine our government at every level working under the same principles. This is exactly what the founders of our country had in mind—citizen-rulers, serving for one or two terms at the most, sharing what wisdom they have in a spirit of public service, and then returning to private life. The idea of a career politician and bureaucrat is as perilous to democracy as the idea of career priests or ministers is to Christianity. Neither will have a place in Zion.

What Can We Do Now?

Having examined the polity, let's turn to the society—for here is where we find the changes that *we* can begin to bring about right now, without elections, without legislation, without further revelation. We don't even have to wait for permission.

Self-Judgment. First, we have to begin by examining ourselves and repenting, if necessary. The first thing we need to discover about ourselves is whether we oppress the poor, and if we do, we need to stop. For example, suppose you're a doctor and, in order to make things run smoothly in your office, you require that people pay cash up front, and if they're going to get Medicaid or Medicare or insurance payments to cover it, it's their responsibility to get their reimbursement from the company or from the government. Now, whom does that hurt? Not people with lots of money. It doesn't bother them at all. You can have that policy as far as they're concerned; they'll just write you a check.

It only hurts the people who can least afford the money. They can't pay cash up front because they don't have the cash. And if you refuse to deal with Medicare or Medicaid, you are saying that those people do not deserve medical care, because they can't get it from you at all.

If this is what you're doing, then you have to recognize the consequences of your actions and honestly say, "Yes, I am oppressing the poor. They *do* suffer because of me." And then you had better stop.

Do you refuse to let your kids associate with ragged children? Then you are teaching them to despise the poor, and building a division into society. And if you say you are keeping them away from poor children in order to protect your kids from crime and evil, just remember how much drugs cost, and remember who buys the most drugs, especially in places like Utah.

Do you make fun of people with poor grammar, or a beat-up car, or flamingoes on their lawn? Then you are lifted up in the pride of your heart and *you* are the one who needs to change before you can possibly help build Zion.

Know What Is Good. The second step is, we need a radical change in values. Teach your children to honor most those who contribute the most to the community, not those who withdraw the most and use it for themselves. We must think of people who devote their lives to acquiring property for exclusive private enjoyment the way we might think of an unpleasant chronic skin disease, easily curable if the sufferer would only *bathe*. We should pity the wealthy and teach our children the worthlessness of their amassing of possessions.

This doesn't mean that no one can buy beautiful things—but it must mean that they don't treasure them, and hoard them, but rather share them with as many as possible, and care for them as part of the public trust. The huge houses on the hills of Salt Lake and Utah valleys are not an offense against God if their many rooms are used to provide temporary homes for the homeless, for widows and orphans, for the weak and fearful, or if they are used by families so large that no smaller space would allow them all to dwell together. But I can't think of a single other case in which they're *not* an offense against God.

The vacation home up in the hills is not an offense against God if it is freely shared with many people who need a retreat from the world.

The sturdy, beautiful foreign car with the flamboyant logo is only a curse to its owner if he isn't willing to lend it or give it away the moment he realizes someone else needs it more.

Know What Is Ours. The third step is, we need a radical change in story. We must come to believe that we don't own our own stuff—and then act on that belief. That's what faith is, of course, what *knowledge* is, in this world where nothing can be known: Knowledge is any belief that we hold so strongly that we act as if it is true; then, as far as society is concerned, it *becomes* true.

Thus we must no longer feel that *we* are the proper ones to decide where to bestow the possessions and goods that the Lord has blessed us with. We should leave that up to the bishop, giving all our surplus to him as contributions to the fast-offering funds of the Church.

A good friend of mine, when she first heard the news of the new policy of drawing ward budgets uniformly out of tithing funds, instantly responded, "Oh, good! That means we can give more to fast offerings!" In her mind, the money still belonged to God. If we all had that attitude, then the fast-offering funds would overflow, and the Church could honestly say that we have no poor among us. In the world's eyes we might all be poor, because no one would "own" anything, and yet in our own eyes we would be rich, because everyone would have enough.

Then we *will* be ready, as a society, for the coming of the Savior, for we will all be acting toward each other as good shepherds; we will know the countenance of the one Good Shepherd, for we will already have seen him in each other's faces, and in each other's lives.

Where Will Zion First Appear?

So far, I've been talking about fitting the Zion ethos into the existing capitalist society of America, and how we might create *here* the polity that will serve the new Zion economy. But the transitions would be hard—and they all presuppose a breakdown of the existing order and constitution of American society. What we must understand is that while we in America are the Saints who have the means to *fund* Zion, our nation may not be the place where the polity of Zion will first come to exist.

The world is very large, and when we have fed and housed all the poor in America, we will hardly have begun to deal with the problem of poverty in the world. We do have the answer, as a church, but we will only succeed in building Zion when we give that answer to people who are desperately asking the question.

Latin America. Let's take a look at Latin America. I think that it is there, especially among the descendants of conquered and enslaved peoples who still feel the repercussions of the conquest and captivity many centuries later, that we might find it possible to establish the first polity of Zion. I think it's possible that out of poverty we might be able to create community. Could there not be LDS communes established in some country or countries of Latin America, where Saints could live either Brigham Young's united order or, preferably, Joseph Smith's law of consecration? Could we not teach the principles of stewardship as an alternative to the totalitarianism of communism?

I think it could be maintained with funding by the sweat of their own brows, even though it would need to be launched with the help of vastly expanded fast-offering money from righteous Saints in America. Perhaps the Shining Path in Peru will still call us their enemy, but it won't be because, as Americans, we are helping to sustain the system that oppresses the people, but rather because, as Saints, we are showing the people, LDS or not, how to establish justice without any need for the violence and hatred of the Shining Path. They would hate us then because we would be achieving the very goals they claim to aim for, without the suffering that their methods invariably cause. Or, perhaps—and this is what I *hope*—they would see our works, put down their guns, pick up their plows, and join us. Then the missionaries killed by terrorists in South America will not have died in vain.

Asia. Another place we might look as a setting for a Zion community is East Asia. The family there is far stronger, society-wide, than here and so, traditionally, is the willingness to sacrifice self-interest for the common good. Our government right now is trying very hard to persuade the Japanese to get their citizens to act more like Americans—more selfish, less dependable, less trusting, less concerned about earning the love and honor of their neighbors and much more concerned about getting more *stuff*. I hope our government fails; I hope that the Church in Asia is building on the foundation of the local traditions, and that we American Saints will learn from them.

Africa. I think Africa, too, *might* be a possible place for Zion societies to grow in the Church. I fear, though, that vast and terrible conflicts are due to arise there soon, since there is no deep strength in the national governments. All of the boundaries in sub-Saharan Africa are artificial, cutting across every natural boundary, every tribal boundary; they are fictions created by European powers for their own purposes, and maintained now by exploitative governments in order to maintain themselves in power. I think the first real wind will blow them down. We see some of that already in South Africa, where the African National Congress represents nationalism and the Zulus, tribalism—neither one quite with purity, but close enough for now. The long struggle against apartheid has made the ANC strong, but in other countries, and in the long run, tribalism is the certain winner. It has a lot more years behind it, a lot more power in the communities. Tribalism won in Nigeria; it's at the heart of slaughter in Rwanda, Burundi, Uganda, Sudan, and Ethiopia; it seethes just under the surface in Kenya, Mozambique, Angola, and Zaire.

In a tribal struggle, I fear that Church members may be seen as traitors to the tribe, and that in the persecution and turmoil of tribal war, no economic experiment could survive where the fires burn hottest. On the other hand, out of trials and persecutions the faithful learn great strength and determination; it may therefore be in Africa that the Church finds its greatest vigor, its greatest unity, and therefore its best chance of developing Zions—wherever peace is established and maintained.

Disinherited People in America. And it is not to be forgotten that there are nations within our own borders that are not and never have been fully participating parts of American society as a whole. I speak of the reservations of Native Americans, where they already have powerful traditions of sharing their possessions with anyone in need, giving their greatest honor to those who share the most with others. Building Zion would not require such a wrenching change of heart among such people.

And in our inner cities, and in places in the rural South, the grandchildren of slaves, who have never fully partaken of the bounty and freedom of America and who are now joining the Church in droves, may provide the core of a genuine Zion community; it has long been true that those who have the least are often those who share the most. We must be prepared, as a church, to encourage the establishment of Zion wherever the Saints want to live it; and in each such place, the Saints must be prepared to embrace the nonmembers who are willing to live the law of the community. Our strength will come from including all who wish to join us.

In all these places, though, inside and outside of the United States, Mormonism must present a new face, one that so far remains invisible. We carefully hold back information about the Church welfare system when we preach the gospel among the poor, so that people won't join the Church for money. But if, instead of welfare, we were preaching the gospel of consecration and Zion, in which participation begins with sacrifice and continues with accountability, then we could be the harbingers of a new economic order, a complete change in their way of life. We could offer a replacement of the shamefully unjust economic system that strangles the people of most of Latin America; and in Africa we would offer a far better modern adaptation of the tribal, clan-centered way of life than capitalism can *ever* offer.

Former Communist Lands. Which brings us to the countries of Eastern Europe, where the Communist Party has lost its intolerable grip. Let us hope and pray that the death of the Communist Party does not also mean the death of the Communist ideal—of fair distribution of the world's goods. It should mean, in fact, the rebirth of that dream, since the Communist Party has been the worst enemy of the Communist ideal the world has ever seen.

Remember that the Communist Party in Eastern Europe was the agent of the conqueror; in the Soviet Union itself, it functioned as the ultimate capitalist monopoly. Under Party rule, you could not work unless you worked for them. *All* jobs were held at the pleasure of the party, and disloyalty was punished by your losing your job, your house, your identity. (In America, you would also have lost your Visa card.) Loyalty, on the other hand, was rewarded with privilege and power. In other words, the Communist Party in the Soviet Union worked on exactly the same principles as the average American corporation. The analogy is nearly perfect, including the KGB and Siberia, as anyone who has worked in the average American corporation knows—both roles are well filled. Russia has long lived under the direction of a self-perpetuating capitalist board of directors with an all-powerful CEO. The current attempt to introduce a free market means introducing competition, which as everyone knows is the *enemy* of capitalism and requires state intervention in the United States to maintain it.

But we Latter-day Saints have a better idea than bringing competition and capitalism to Russia and the newly free nations of Eastern Europe. We can, if we want to, enter the Soviet Union with the gospel of fairness and equity, the gospel of Zion. We can bring them, through the gospel of Jesus Christ, the fulfillment of all the ideals that the Communist Party betrayed. What could not be achieved by appealing to atheism *can* be achieved in the name of Christ. What could not be forced on people by blood and terror *can* be given to them freely in love and trust.

But the Church can't preach consecration until the Saints live it. And, as with so many other doctrines, the Saints will never begin to live it just because someone has commanded them to. Anyone who has worked in Church government knows *that* very well. The world thinks that we are puppets—the prophet speaks and everybody moves exactly as he says that we should. The truth is quite different. Anybody who has actually tried to get anybody in any ward to change the way they do things *knows* that section 121 is right—"no power or influence can or ought to be maintained by virtue of the Priesthood, only by persuasion, by *long*-suffering." The Saints will only live the law of consecration when we as a people want to, when we desire righteousness, when we've been taught the correct principles that will bring true charity into our lives.

When Zion Is Found Again in the World

What will Zion accomplish? The abolition of hunger, poverty, illiteracy throughout the world; it will bring the entire world into the community of light. Our economic order will spread faster than the gospel. Once we have established Zion in one place, there will be people begging us to send them bishops—the missionaries will bring the bishop with them, instead of waiting years before he comes. We can be the means by which the human community is healed and made one.

Zion will also accomplish the healing of the planet. Our living

Earth—the rocks, the soil, the oceans, the atmosphere, and all the creatures that dwell therein—have been poisoned. Zion will remove the element of competition that is killing them. Brazil won't feel a need to turn its rain forests into cattle ranches, because the Brazilian people will know that tending the rain forest is their stewardship, and that if they fulfill that stewardship well, they will have just as large a share of the wealth of the world as any other nation. They don't know that now because it isn't true, and so it makes no sense for them to stop cutting down the trees. But when they *do* have that trust, there's no reason for them to cut them down at all.

And finally, the result of a world-wide Zion is the universal communion of God and man. We will not become holy because Christ comes to dwell among us; Christ will come to dwell among us because we are so much in harmony with each other and with the world our Savior gave us that he will feel as much at home with us as in heaven. He has already taught us all we need to know to create a city and a nation and a world where "Holiness to the Lord" is written, truthfully, over every doorway. The Earth will not become a Urim and Thummim to us until every home and office, every factory and school is a temple to the Most High God.

Where does it begin? It begins here. It begins today. Now. In your heart. If *you* begin to live the law of consecration, not waiting for anybody else; if *you* begin, not just by telling yourself that all you have belongs to God, but by acting it out in your life, then we are that much closer to Zion. And as far as it's in your power, you will have prepared the world for the coming of Christ.

Now, how can you do that? I've said it before, in other places, and so have many other people. Simply stated, you do what it says in the Doctrine and Covenants—you turn your surplus over to the bishop. As with tithing, your conscience must teach you what your surplus is.

Just as examples: If when you're shopping for clothes for your kids, you find yourself going for the designer rack for the clothes with the "cool" labels, then maybe that's the time for you to decide that you don't *need* that, and instead you will buy something a little cheaper but still of adequate quality. Then take the money you *would* have spent and give it to the bishop.

Or, again: You're tempted to buy a fancy new recreational vehicle, because, after all, that's the life you've always dreamed of living. But then, what if you took that money and gave it to the bishop, maybe helping somebody else to live in a decent house?

Or, perhaps you want to buy a "great" car. But instead you buy something that's practical and simple, and then you go to the bishop and offer to buy somebody else an equally practical car with the money you just saved.

Even if you don't buy a lot of expensive things, you can begin by simply deciding not to sell your used things whenever you are through with them. Instead, give the used item away wherever it's needed. If you haven't personally noticed a need, then go to the bishop or to the Relief Society president and ask them who might need it. Better yet, simply ask them *if* somebody needs it, then give it to them to give away without even worrying about who will end up with it.

However you dispose of your surplus, you must never look on those old possessions as if you had some claim on them, as if it's your place to decide whether the bishop or the Relief Society president used them wisely. Those things were never yours in the first place—you were only their steward for a time.

Do these things, and Zion will soon exist in your home. You and your children will thrive in righteousness, and Satan will have no power over you.

Now, on the other hand, if you put off your obedience to the law of consecration, if you figure that you'll start to live a consecrated life when you have a little more money ahead, or when your neighbors start doing it, or when your career is more firmly established—then *you* are part of the reason that the world is in bondage and suffering. As far as it's within your power, you will have aided the enemies of righteousness and conspired with them to keep the Savior from walking openly among his brothers and sisters.

All that has been said about Zion, here and elsewhere, is nothing but theory, nothing but wind and empty argument, until we choose to act. No hierarchy or government can ever create Zion. No hands can deliberately hew it out of the stones of the world. But you can start living now as if Zion were already here, bestowing trust even where trust is not yet deserved, sharing your plenty even when by the world's deceitful standards you do not have "enough." By the world's standards, you can *never* have enough; by God's standards, you already do.

I once wrote a play based on the story of the Salt Lake City businessman during the time of Brigham Young who was called into the prophet's office and assigned to go on a "rag mission"—collecting rags from the Saints so that they could use them to make paper to print the *Deseret News*. This was a businessman, for heaven's sake; he was supposed to be a stake president, not a rag-picker! But after some inner struggle he said yes, and he went, and he discovered the most amazing thing: The rich so often had nothing to spare, and when they did they only had room for him to stand in the kitchen to eat quickly and then hurried him away. But the poor, apparently, were in much better shape, because they could always find room for him to sit at the family table, where they would give him food from the common pot, as big a share as anyone, or bigger. They always seemed to have a warm, dry space for him to lie down and sleep.

If enough of us turn our hearts and lives toward our God and toward our sisters and brothers, then the hierarchies and the governments of the world will be caught up in the great stone cut without hands from the mountain of the Lord's house, and without compulsory means it will roll forth and fill the Earth.

That is the vision we have been given, over and over. I know it's true. Wherever I've found Saints living this way, I've seen that their lives are filled with joy, and everyone whose life is touched by these Zion people is blessed. It's not only conceivable, it's not only possible, it's not only desirable—it is also the will of our loving Father that we receive this gift by giving it to each other and to the whole world. It's time to grow up and together, as one heart, one soul, one child of God, inherit the kingdom that he has offered to us all along.

Acknowledgments

Years ago, I worked for a time with Scott Kenney, the man most responsible for *Sunstone* magazine in its early days; later, when Scott became the editor of Signature Books, we were associated on several projects. Even though there were many matters on which we did not see eye to eye, we were able to work together well because of our mutual respect; we knew that even in disagreement, we were both trying in good faith to contribute some truth and light, as best we could understand it, to the community of Saints. It was a time of sacrifice, and Scott more than anyone else I know gave selflessly to the Mormon community—even at times when some members of the Mormon community weren't quite sure they wanted to accept the gifts he was offering.

Scott brought out the best in me at that time, forcing me to think my ideas through to their conclusions and then giving me a chance in the pages of *Sunstone* and in projects with the early Signature Books to express some of my ideas and attitudes. During that time he suggested to me earnestly that I should write a book of essays. I felt flattered that a man like Scott Kenney would think that such a book would have value to an audience, and though at the time I hadn't the confidence to proceed with the project, his suggestion lingered with me in the back of my mind. As opportunities came to write or speak, I prepared my words with the idea that someday they might be offered in book form. So even though Scott is not connected with this book now, his early confidence in me and our years of close association are at the root of the book. That's why it is dedicated to him; that, and because in my heart he is still a dear and honored friend.

Others, of course, have helped greatly. Elbert Peck, the current editor of *Sunstone*, was the one who gave me the chance to write an intermittent column for that magazine for several years. I came to him in the *Sunstone* offices to protest the magazine's inclusion of a letter to the editor calling for people to contribute accounts of their spiritual experiences with "Mother God." "Elbert," I said, "if someone wrote a letter to the editor calling for accounts of spiritual experiences with living in polygamy today, you wouldn't have run *that*, would you?" While I have no idea if I made Elbert regret having run the letter that bothered me (he may merely have regretted coming back from lunch that day), I do know that our conversation turned to my perception that *Sunstone* had been captured by what I then called the Mormon Left, and what I now refer to as assimilationists. Elbert protested that he would gladly publish more articles and essays from the mainstream of the Church, but "we can't publish articles we don't get." Then he added, "If you want to see more material in *Sunstone* that reflects an orthodox view, why don't you write for us?"

So I began writing my column, "A Changed Man"; many of the essays in this book had their first publication in the pages of Elbert Peck's magazine. Elbert never flinched from publishing what I wrote, even when he took enormous amounts of flack from the *Sunstone* audience for having done so. While *Sunstone* is not today the magazine that I had hoped it would become when I worked on it in its early days and when I contributed to it more recently, I remain of the opinion that Elbert Peck is a genuinely fair-minded editor who truly cares about the Mormon community and seeks to help the Mormon people to grow. May his tribe increase.

I also owe thanks to Garry Garff, whose superb editing of this book improved it greatly. I have no intention of telling anyone the mistakes that Garry prevented me from making; instead, thanks to Garry, I will seem to be a much wiser and more careful writer than I actually am. It was also Garry who assembled many of the essays that appear here, some of which I had forgotten that I even wrote. And it was Garry who proposed that Bookcraft publish this book in the first place; without him, it would not exist.

My mother, Peggy Card, transcribed the speeches that are included here; if you heard some of the muddy-sounding passages that she managed to decipher, you might wonder if perhaps she had a seerstone of her own to aid in the translation. My assistant, Kathleen Bellamy, also retyped many of these essays from xeroxes of the original publications.

I also thank those whose invitation to speak provided me with a chance to develop my ideas before an audience, including Lanny Britsch, Scott Samuelson, Harold Oaks, and the dedicated science fiction fans at BYU who put on the annual "Symposium on Life, the Universe, and Everything." Above all, I thank my wife Kristine; it is in conversation with her that all my thoughts are first expressed; her natural skepticism is the first hurdle my ideas must clear; her questions and suggestions improve everything I write; and her encouragement and help are the foundation of everything I achieve.

About the Author

Orson Scott Card, an internationally acclaimed writer of science fiction and fantasy, is the author of the *Ender's Game* saga, *The Tales of Alvin Maker* series, the *Homecoming* saga, and many other novels, stories, essays, and plays. He is the first author to win the prestigious Hugo and Nebula awards for best novel two years in a row—for *Ender's Game* and its sequel *Speaker for the Dead.* Also, he writes a column on Mormonism for Beliefnet (located at www.beliefnet.com), an Internet site that discusses various religions. A former assistant editor for the *Ensign* magazine, he received degrees from Brigham Young University and the University of Utah. He and his wife, Kristine, are the parents of five children. They live in Greensboro, North Carolina.